Heaven
OR
Hell

WHICH WILL YOU CHOOSE?

GERALDINE M. COOL

 www.trafford.com
North America & international
toll-free: 1 888 232 4444 (USA & Canada)
fax: 812 355 4082

FOREWORD

RIFTING, DRIFTING INTO THE abyss of darkness with not a speck of light to be seen. I was given this experience to show me that my life was not my own and I had no right to try and take it. Through the suicide attempts God's hand was upon me because he saw something within me that he knew could be saved. God has been gracious to me and seen me though many trials. Finally I put my faith in God and let him take control and my life is much happier.

As you read this book think about the things that you have done either good or bad. Thank God for the good things and pray to him to release and cleanse you from the bad things. This is my prayer for each and every one of you.

GOD BLESS

INTRODUCTION

I DECIDED TO WRITE THIS book because of all the lost souls in the world that need the saving grace of God and need to know there is a heaven and a hell. What I experienced on my journey will have you thinking twice about your destination. Heaven or Hell, these are the only two places after death. I do not want anyone to go though the experiences I did just to learn that there are chooses we need to make and that each chose has its consequences. There are tortures and torments in store for you if you chose hell and there is really a lake of fire in Hell. Heaven is peaceful, calm and full of joy.

This journey was necessary for me because of my foolish behavior in thinking I could take my own life. I am so thankful that God had other plans for me. I am a child of God and walk in his footsteps each and every day.

CHAPTER 1

RIFTING, DRIFTING INTO THE abyss of darkness. The bottle of anti-depressants was sending me into a new world. I was no longer of this world, only darkness overtaking me. *Suddenly,* within a blink of an eye, I felt free and light. Looking around me I saw a woman lying in a hospital room with doctors and nurses working fervently over her. As I watched this scene I was approached by two men in *red* telling me to come with them. I stood hesitantly! Before I could decide whether or not to go with them, one grabbed one arm and the other man grabbed the other. They led me to a place that was beautiful beyond words. This is *Heaven!!* As far as the eye could see, there was a big, brilliantly shining wall. Within the wall, I noticed two doors; one door was long but closed. The other was large, black and ominous. Along the wall were two chairs—one was fairly large and the other much smaller and both were made of pure gold. Glancing to my left, I beheld *Paradise* with majestic trees, a crystal clear waterfall and the most beautiful green grass I had ever seen.

The most glorious sight was my Heavenly Father standing in front of me. Because of the brilliance remitting from his face I could not make out his features. His brilliance reminded me of a verse in Revelation 21: 23: ". . . the city had no need of sun . . . for the glory of God did lighten it . . ." now here I stood in front of the brilliance. All of heaven shone and was made bright from the light. His body I did not see—at the same time I saw his body was with the Son. They were inside, intertwined, within each other. They were together, yet at the same time there was a separation in them—but still one.

On either side of the Heavenly Father were two angels, Gabriel and Michael. Their names, I knew for they, were written on their foreheads in gold.

Standing in the presence of God, I felt so dirty. Falling on my knees, I cried because I was so ashamed of myself. Reaching his hand out to me, God lifted me to my feet and motioned for me to sit in the smaller chair. Almost immediately a movie begin to play and before long I realized it was of my life from conception to the present. Nearing the end of the movie, he turned to me and said: "Child, the most important part was after you were saved." I professed to be a Christian but I didn't show the fruits, going my own way.

With eyes full of pain, for me, he said *Hell is your Destiny.* Gabriel grabbed me by the arm and with some force, for I did not want to go, led me to black, ugly door. I wanted to stop myself, but couldn't, because I was in the spirit realm. As we neared the door it opened and I was led through it. The darkness on this side, of the door, was so overwhelming I could not see myself. Total darkness enveloped me. Suddenly, it seemed like the bottom of where we were standing broke open. Faster and faster, like a whirlwind, we fell. The temperature got hotter and hotter the farther we fell. I closed my eyes for I didn't want to see where we were.

With a sudden jolt we stopped. Upon impact I opened my eyes and found we were on a great road, fearful of the uncertainty of where it led. Thirst was overwhelming. I'm thirsty—I'm thirsty I kept telling Gabriel but he acted as if he didn't hear me. Starting to cry, the tears fell down my cheeks but were instantly evaporated. Suddenly the smell of sulfur permeated me. It reminded me of burning tires. Covering my nose only made it worse. All my senses were sensitive to this smell.

I looked down at my arms and all the hair had disappeared. Oh! The heat—it was hot-hot-hot.

As I looked around I could see people tormented by demons. One lady in particular caught my attention because of her suffering that the demon was inflicting upon her. This tormenting demon would cut the woman's head off and then with a spear (dagger) would stab her throughout her entire body. Eyes, body, feet, hands, legs, arms were continually stabbed. The eyes of the demon were demonic and filled with evil—eyes of someone who didn't care. When he had run out of places to stab, he would put the woman's head back on and start the onslaught again. The scream from this woman were agonizing to listen to.

Slightly tilting my head I saw a man, probably in his 20's, which was being tormented by another demon. Around his neck was and he was standing in front of a fire pit. This demon was also armed with a spear and with this spear he would stab the young man over and over again on every part of his body. With the chain that was around his neck the demon would hurl the young man into the pit of fire, repeating this over and over. While the young man was in the pit I could not hear him, but once he was pulled out, his screams were excruciating. The sound was so excruciating that I covered my ears but the sound still penetrated through. It seemed my hearing was more sensitive.

The first two demons were ugly but the third one I seen was, by far, the ugliest, hideous, frightful creature I had ever seen. His body had the characteristics of many animals and to explain it further I cannot do. His goal was to scare anyone who looked at him, which is exactly what happened. People were scared beyond description.

The next demon I saw was so beautiful, looking like he could be an angel of God, but he wasn't. For the difference between the angels of God and the demons were that the demons did not have their names written on their foreheads as the angels of God did.

The angel Gabriel looked up as I glanced back. My thought was that he did not want to see the poor souls being tortured. My thought was "Why is he still here. Aren't I supposed to be waiting for my turn to be tortured?"

Suddenly thirst overtook me and I said to Gabriel that I was thirsty.

With tenderness in his eyes that I hadn't seen before he told me that the Lord had decided to give me another chance. My heart jumped for joy and instantly the thirst, the agony and hurting went away. I felt peaceful.

As Gabriel took my hand and we were about to rise above this hell, I heard my name called. Holly Jo, Holly Jo, help me, help me. Looking around I tried to see where the voice was coming from but the flames blocked her face. The only thing I seen was her hands stretched out wanting me to help her. My heart's desire was to help her, I knew I couldn't. My hands went right through hers. As much as my heart desired to help her, I knew I couldn't because she had no hope. There was no way I could help her.

In this hideous place I seen family, friends and other people I knew. Their faces looked familiar but were obscured beyond recognition. The only way I knew them was by their characteristics. Seeing family, friends from school, church and home being tormented and tortured in this place really hurt deeply. I had not known their lives. I thought—maybe the bad testimony that I was giving them, saying I was a Christian, but yet living my own way, was the reason they did not know God and as a result they turned away from God. Could it possibly be my fault that they were there? My head kept spinning with this thought.

In hell there is no time, no past, no future—everything is the same. These people were destined to be there. I saw these people on my visit to hell, but thank God, these people are still alive today.

Finally Gabriel and I ascended back into the presence of God. I fell upon my knees before him and cried, because I was ashamed of myself and I could not look upon his face.

With a voice sweeter than honey he said to me 'Holly Jo, I love you.' I never thought anyone could love me. But just by the tone of his voice I knew that these words came directly from his heart. Anyone that calls him Father, he will love. Taking my face in his hands he lifted my head so I was looking directly into his face. 'Holly Jo, I love you.'

Looking deeply into his eyes it was as if there was a movie screen playing showing me many things. For one, the earth surrounded by a soft like ozone layer. It looked as soft as clouds, so I reached up and touched them. Upon touching the softness I realized it was the

Holy Spirit because it baptized me and then I began speaking in other tongues.

During this time I saw and felt evil spirits coming out of my body. I was being cleansed. Overdosing on pills not only messed up my mind but it opened doors for evil spirits to enter. Each overdose brought in more evil spirits which tormented me unmercifully. Under the influence of these drugs the way I acted was not really me but the evil spirits inside me.

John 1: 29: ". . . Behold the Lamb of God, which taketh away the sin of the world."

Thank God when I was saved my house was cleansed. When I was baptized I saw these spirits leave. First there were seven, then seven more and then another seven and they kept multiplying until I could not count them. Matthew 12: 43-45: "When an evil spirit comes out of a person, it travels through dry places, looking for a place to rest, but it doesn't find it. So the spirit says I will go back to the house I left. When the spirit comes back, it finds the house still empty, swept clean and made neat. Then the spirit goes out and brings seven other spirits even more evil than it is, and they go in and live there. So the person has even more trouble than before . . ." Thank the Lord they were all cleansed from me.

The Lord gave me a glimpse of the events leading up to the rapture for each day brings us closer and closer. *The rapture is near.*

Examine yourself—then ask yourself this question—*Am I ready to meet the Lord?*

Warning—warning, the rapture is near.

Joel 2: 28 tell us in the last days your sons and daughters will prophesy—your old men will dream dreams and your young men will see visions. This is one of the last prophecies that haven't been fulfilled.

There are multitudes of young people who are rising up and preaching the word of God.

Satan (the devil) is trying hard to form an army of young people but the Lord is more powerful.

If you are really serious about accepting the Lord and truly want to serve him then he will give you strength to overcome Satan (the devil) so that you will be able to preach his word far and wide—as he commanded in the Bible.

2 Corinthians 6: 2: ". . . now is the accepted time; behold now is the day of salvation."

Hebrews 4: 7: ". . . Today if ye hear his voice harden not your hearts."

The Lord told me he had a mission for me and that mission was to share his love with all I met. That is one commandment I will complete.

With no fanfare of any kind, no tunnels to pass through, no darkness I suddenly woke up in a hospital bed with IV's dripping into my arm, a heart monitor checking my heart and an oxygen monitor on my finger. I learned that a nurse had been ordered to keep vigil by my bedside the whole night through. All my vitals had bottomed out and I was not expected to live. It was at this point that I had left my body. With the slight movement from me, she was instantly at my side. There was compassion in this nurse's face and she told me she had been very worried about me. Several times during the night all vitals would drop to a dangerous level, and then improve a little. The last time, before returning to consciousness, she told me I said I did not want to return. This statement really worried her. Foam spilled from my mouth and I babbled words no one could understand.

My sister walked into the room and I could tell she was worried about me, but at the same first she was upset over what I had done. She sat by the side of my bed and explained to me that the pastor of our church had found me unconscious on the floor and had rushed me to the hospital along with the empty bottle of anti-depressants. Before returning to my body the Lord told me I had to tell my sister everything, which I did.

Family members, I beseech you, never, ever stop praying for the *lost sheep* of the family. In Matthew 8: 12 we are told that the shepherd left the rest of his herd and went to seek the one lost sheep.

A message for everyone—examine yourself. Ask yourself; "Why should I care what anyone says about me?" That was my problem—I was always concerned of what people said about me. I often worried about what others were thinking about me, but now I realize that they really didn't care about me. When I stand before the Lord they will not be there. No family, friends, no pastor, no one from the church will be there to help me. *Alone* I will stand before God defending myself. Each and every one of us must stand before the Lord—alone. God is Holy, Heaven is holy and a feeling of not belonging there filled my soul because I was in sin.

2 Corinthians 6: 2: ". . . behold, now is the accepted time; behold now is the day of salvation." Accept the Lord today and *do not delay.* This will be the most important decision of your life. What I say is not meant to scare you into heaven, but it is said to show you the mercy and love God has for you. Christ died to save us from our sins. Matthew 1: 21 ". . . for he will save His people from their sins." Galatians 1: 4: "Who gave himself for our sins . . . ?" Each drop of his blood was shed for the forgiveness of our sins.

I beseech each and every one who reads this book to come to the Lord and never fear what anyone says about you.

Serve the Lord with all your heart. Joshua 24: 15: ". . . choose you this day whom you will serve . . ." Romans 12: 1: "I beseech you therefore brethren, by the mercies of God, that ye present your bodies a living sacrifice, holy, acceptable unto God, which is your reasonable service." Don't just say it with your mouth, but say it with your heart and mind. Matthew

22: 37: "Love the Lord your God with all your heart, all your soul and all your mind."

Do not worry about tomorrow, for tomorrow may never come. Death may come knocking at your door.

Think about it!!! Our lives are not our own-we are on borrowed time—for our lives belong to God.

We as mortal human beings take advantage by not caring, going into the world and doing things of the world. Sure the world has a lot to offer but the Lord has so much more to offer.

Believe it or not—there is a Heaven and a Hell. I know I have journeyed to both.

God is eternal life. Eternal life is forever.

If you want to accept Jesus as your Savior, bow your head and pray this prayer—"Lord God, in the precious name of Jesus, I want to accept you as my Savior, this very moment. Come into my life, Lord Jesus. Cleanse me of my sins and make me whiter than snow. Hell is real and I don't want to go there. For everything I have done, forgive me. I reveal to you every little secret and ask forgiveness of them all. My Lord, I believe you died on the cross and that you rose from the dead. Come into my heart be and reign within my heart. Reading your word will be a priority and I will be more in your word. Amen. I will strive to attend church regularly because it will be a help mate to me because I know you are there."

Matthew 18: 20: ". . . where two or three are gathered together in my name, there am I in the midst of them." I know, Lord, you will be there with us.

Lord, my hearts desires to be where you are.

Welcome to the kingdom of heaven, if you prayed the sinners prayed. Now you are a brother or sister to other Christian believers.

Don't take advantage of this most important decision of your life. Do not go back into your old way of living or Satan will again have you in his grasp. Satan and the world leads to death, but God leads to eternal life. Live like it were your last day and the last chance to ask forgiveness.

If this testimony has touched your heart, pass it on to friends, family or anyone else who needs a touch from God. Share with others so they may accept Christ as their Savior.

Please do not let a moment pass by—because it could be your last moment.

Has God ever spoken personally to you? God does speak and he is real. Often it takes a tragedy to humble us. Men by nature tend to be quite proud.

Remember one thing—

Whatever you do in your life, wherever you go, no matter how far you think you've gone away from God, remember this one thing. If you are in trouble and in need, cry out to God from your heart and he will hear you. He really hears you and will forgive you.

Do you believe in God?

Lord, I ask you to forgive me of my sins and for the things I have done wrong—which are many. They're wrong. I know they're wrong because my conscience tells me they are wrong. If you can forgive me of all my sins, I don't know how you can do it, I have no idea how you can forgive them—but please forgive me of my sins. Wipe my slate clean so I may start anew. Forgive me, Lord.

I know, Lord, that I need to forgive those who have hurt me. Let me stop and say I forgive you to each person that comes to mind.

Lord, if you can forgive them, can I do any less. I will forgive them.

I have no idea what your will is—I do know that it is not to do evil things—but other than that I have no idea what your will is.

1 John 1: 9: "If we confess our sins, he is faithful and just to forgive us our sins and to cleanse us from all unrighteousness." Lord, cleanse me and forgive me for the wickedness and evil doing. For all who have hurt me, I forgive them. Jesus, I will do your will for I want your will to be done in my life and I will follow you.

Ecclesiastes 12: 7: "Then shall the dust return to the earth as it was: and the spirit shall return unto God who gave it."

I was standing there, but without a body. There was a sensation and a feeling of a body, but nothing physical to touch. My physical body was dead and I was a spiritual being. I was very much alive, aware that I had legs, arms and a head, but I could no longer touch them. God is a spirit, an invisible spiritual being and we are created in his image.

Genesis 1: 26: "Let us make man in our image, after our likeness . . ."

As I stood there I felt a penetrating coldness and fear come over me. In the darkness I sensed there was evil. The darkness seemed not just physical but spiritual.

"Where am I?—Where am I?"

I sensed I was being watched for the air around me became filled with a cold, encroaching evil that seemed to prevail. This evil surrounded me. I became aware of other people moving around me in the same predicament, as myself. They answered my thoughts without me uttering a word. The voices in the darkness were screaming; "Shut up, you deserve to be here."

The sudden realization that I was in hell startled me. Could this actually be real—how did I end up here? This realization terrified me so much that I was afraid to speak or move. As I looked back over my life I thought; 'Yep, I could have deserved this place.'

Hell is the most frightening place a person could ever be. People here cannot do anything their evil heart's desire—nothing at all. There is nothing good in hell to talk about. *NOTHING!!* These people knew judgment was coming. In the book of Jude, verse 6 it states ". . . he hath reserved in everlasting chains under darkness under darkness unto the judgment of the great day." And in verse 7 it says "They suffer the punishment of eternal fire, for all to see." Verse 15 ". . . He is coming to punish all who are against God for the evil they have done against him. And he will punish the sinners who are against God for all the evil they have said against him."

There is no relationship in time for in hell people cannot tell time. Hell is a very frightening place. The Bible tells us there are two kingdoms—the kingdom of darkness and the kingdom of light. In the book of Jude it tells us the place of darkness was actually prepared for the angels who disobeyed God, not for the people, ever.

2 Thessalonians 1: 9: "Those people will be punished with a destruction that continues forever. They will be kept away from the Lord and from his great power."

Hell is the most frightening, horrifying, disgusting and frightening place and no way would I ever wish my enemies to go there.

Matthew 23: 33: ". . . How are you going to escape God's judgment?"

Once you are in hell, there is no way out unless you have repented and ask for forgiveness before death. The Bible teaches us that no one can pray for the dead departed souls and get them out of hell. Before death they must have repented.

Suddenly I was drawn out of the darkness by a brilliant light.

1 John 2: 8: ". . . darkness is passing away and the true light is already shining."

Colossians 1: 13: "God has freed us from the power of darkness . . ."

The Bible tells us that a great light shines into darkness, on those walking in the shadow of death and darkness and guides their feet into the paths of peace and righteousness. Piercing through the darkness, an amazing beam of light shone on my face.

I began to feel the weightlessness overwhelm me as the light enveloped me. Being lifted off the ground I began to ascend into this beautiful, brilliant light. As I ascended I was being drawn into a large circular shaped opening and at the other end of the tunnel was light. This light was more brilliant than the sun, more radiant than a diamond, brighter than a laser beam. But the amazing thing was I could look right into it. I felt if I looked back to the way I had come, I would be drawn back into the darkness. My heart jumped with joy to be out of the darkness.

As I traveled through the tunnel, thick intense light emanated with successive waves. As I felt the first wave it brought warmth and control. Not long after the first wave another wave engulfed me giving me complete and total peace. This was something I had been searching for in my life but could never achieve it. Searching for peace of mind I had tried drugs, education, self-inflictions, numerous relationships, with men, but never finding peace.

As the waves of light penetrated my body, from the top of my head to the soles of my feet, I finally found myself at peace.

What does my body look like, I wondered, now that I was in the light? I glanced down and could see my arm but amazingly I could see right through it. I stood there transparent as a spirit, but my body was full of light that had shown on me in the tunnel. I was full of light.

Total joy was the third wave that penetrated my body. What an awesome, exciting experience.

As I stepped from the tunnel I was met by the source of the light and power. A verse in Colossians 1: 13 came to mind. It says; "Who has delivered us from the power of darkness . . ."

My whole vision field was taken up with this incredible light. I immediately thought of it as an aura, then glory.

1 John 1: 5: "God is light and in him is no darkness at all." Christ died on the cross, rose from the dead and ascended into heaven and is now seated at the right hand of the Father. He is glorified and surrounded by light and in him there is no darkness. Jesus is the King of Glory, Prince of Peace, Lord of Lords and King of all Kings. I myself was able to see this incredible light and glory.

As I stood there thinking, a voice spoke to me from the center of the light. It said to me; 'Child, do you wish to return?' It surprised me that someone in the center of the light knew my name. It seemed as though this person could hear my inner thoughts.

Return? Return to where? Where am I? Behind me the tunnel was disappearing into the darkness.

Is this real?

Am I really standing here?

The Lord spoke and said; 'Child, do you wish to return?'

I replied that I did want to return.

If you wish to return, you must see in a new light. Inside my heart and soul something clicked as he spoke the words—see in a new light. I had received Christmas cards saying 'Jesus is the light of the world and God is light and there is no darkness in him.'

I had been shown darkness—but here there certainly was no darkness.

Ephesians 3: 19: "May you experience the love of Christ, though it is so great you will never fully understand it. Then you will be filled with the fullness of the Life and power that comes from God."

Psalms 36:9: ". . . in thy light shall we see light."

1 John 2: 8: ". . . the darkness is past and the true light now shineth."

There is a God and He is light. John 5: 35: "He was a burning and shining light . . ."

He knew my name and my every thought that was in my heart and soul. God was able to see everything I had done in my life, which left me feeling exposed and transparent before him. Feeling ashamed I thought a mistake had been made and the wrong person had been brought up. I'm not a good person and I felt like I should crawl under a rock or go back into the darkness where I belonged. Slowly I started inching my way backs towards the tunnel, but a wave of light emanated forth from God and surrounded me. My heart filled with fear that this light was going to cast me back into the pit. But to my astonishment a wave of pure, unconditional love flowed over me. I never expected anything like that. Instead of judgment I was being cleansed with pure love.

Pure, unadulterated, clean, uninhibited, undeserved love. From the inside out it filled me. My thought was perhaps God doesn't know everything I had done wrong. I started telling him of all the disgusting things I did in cover of darkness. But!!! It was as though he had already forgiven me and the intensity of his love increased. God showed me that when I had ask for forgiveness lying on the hospital bed that he had forgiven me and washed my heart and soul clean from evil.

As this love flowed over and through me it became stronger and stronger and it caused me to weep uncontrollably. There were no strings attached with this clean and pure love.

Jeremiah 31: 3 says that God ". . . loved thee with an everlasting love . . ." Then in John 3: 16 we are told "For God so loved the world that he gave his only begotten Son, that whosoever believeth in him should not perish but have everlasting life."

For decades I had felt unloved and now this love was flowing through me. The only time I felt unconditional love was from my grandfather who died when I was eight. After that my life was only existence, with no one to love me unconditionally. There were things that I thought were love but were not. Sex wasn't love, for that only burnt me up, making me feel dirty and worthless—lust was a raging fire inside me, an uncontrollable desire that burnt every fiber of my being from the inside out.

Standing there the waves of light stopped and I found myself covered completely in this pure light and filled with love. ***STILLNESS!!!***

I thought to myself—could I step into the light that surrounds God and see him face to face. Seeing him face to face I would know the truth.

1 Corinthians 13: 12: ". . . Now we see a dim reflection, as if we were looking into a mirror, but then we shall see clearly. Now I know only a part, but then I will know fully, as God has known me."

Hearing lies and deceptions make me sick. The truth is very important to me.

I had talked to others trying to find the truth of the meaning of life, truth and what's going on.

Something somewhere had to be the truth. Stepping through and seeing God I would know the truth and the meaning of life. That way I would never have to ask anyone ever again.

Could I step in? A voice from somewhere said 'No.' I ignored the voice and stepped through and found myself inside of veils of shimmering light which seemed like suspended diamonds. These diamonds gave off the most astonishing brilliance. The light penetrated my body healing the deepest recesses, my broken inner woman (man) and healing my broken heart.

In the brightest part of the light stood a man dressed in a dazzling white robe reaching to his ankles. This dazzling robe was not made of any earthly material. Oh! No, this robe was a *garment of light.*

I lifted my eyes toward this brilliance and saw a man with arms outstretched in a welcoming gesture. The face on this man was so bright—ten times brighter than any light I had ever seen. What a fantastic light. The sun looked pale yellow compared to the brilliance on his face. Because of the brightness of his face his features were obscured. There was no fear for I could sense a purity and holiness emanating from this light. This light gave me the assurance that I was standing in the presence of the Almighty God— no one but God could look like this. This purity and holiness continually came forth from his face. As this wonderful, bright light emitted from his face it entered me. There was no fear only total freedom and an immense desire to get closer to his face filled my heart.

Only a few feet from him I stood trying to look into the light that surrounded him. Overwhelming me was this fantastic light which was brighter than the sun shining on a field of snow. As I made my way towards him he stepped aside and the light went with him. Behind him was the circular tunnel I had traveled through. Before my eyes I could see a whole new world and an overwhelming feeling that I was standing on the edge of Paradise swept over me, as I glimpsed into eternity.

Titus 1: 2: ". . . the hope for life forever, which God promised to us before time, began."

The beauty in Paradise was completely untouched. Green fields and meadows were in front of me. The grass gave off the same light and life that had been in the presence of God. This grass had a life of its own, springing back after being stepped on. Every plant, flower and tree was disease free. As I looked toward the middle of the meadow I could see a clear stream winding its way through lines of trees. In the distance there were mountains and the sky was blue and clear. Turning slightly I saw rolling green hills and flowers which radiated with a beautiful kaleidoscope of color.

Paradise!!

From the depths of my heart I knew I belonged here. I had finally found what I had been looking for. It gave me the feeling of being born the first time.

Every fiber of my being knew I was home. Never was there so much calmness or peacefulness within me. Just a step away stood eternity.

Jesus stepped in front of the doorway as I took a step towards it. Jesus is the door, the door of life.

John 10: 9: "I am the door . . ."

John 14: 6: ". . . I am the way, the truth and the life: no man cometh unto the Father, but by me."

Christ is the only way. Leading into His kingdom there is only one way which is a narrow passageway and only a few find it. Multitudes of people would rather take the expressway to hell.

As I stood there I heard my glorious Savior ask: 'My dear, precious child, do you wish to return?' in my mind I was screaming; 'Of course not.' Why would I want to return to misery, hatred, despair, gloom, heartaches and uncertainties? For me there was nothing to return for. While on earth I did not get the love that should have been mine; someone to really love me. Standing before Jesus and his light I was surrounded by love and it felt, oh, so good. All I wanted to do was to step through the door to eternity. But the Lord blocked my way and wouldn't move even after I pleaded with him to stay. I was sure that I would be allowed admittance, so I looked down towards earth and said 'Good-bye cruel world, you are no longer my home. I have found something better.'

Within a split second I saw a clear picture of my mother in front of me. Deep down inside I knew she loved me and wanted only what was best for me. I could see the hurt in her eyes and the tears she shed. I knew, deep down inside, that there wasn't a day that went by that she didn't lift a special, silent prayer for her lost and wayward daughter. Being rebellious and headstrong I did not want to listen to her nor did I want to live right. My heart was filled with pride and arrogance. Your ways are leading you into the pits of hell, she would tell me. That did not scare me and I went on living in my sinful ways, doing my own thing no matter who it hurt. Oh! How I had hurt the heart of the woman who had carried and gave me life. She would continually remind me that after death there are only two chooses—heaven or hell. It wasn't until later in life that I knew she was right. As I stood there contemplating, I realized it would be selfish, of me, to go into paradise and leave my mother believing I went to hell. There would be no way of her knowing that I had repented of my sins, on my death bed, and had received Jesus as my Lord and Savior.

Finally I spoke and said, 'Lord, I want to go back for mother's sake. I want her to know that I believe in the living God, that there is a heaven and a hell, that Jesus Christ is the door in which we may enter in.'

Behind my mother were my father, sisters, brothers, friends and many other people. I really believed the Lord was showing me that there was a multitude of people that didn't know and would never know that I was now a child of God and he had saved me from my sins, unless I shared his saving grace, his glorious, wonderful working power with them.

'Lord, who are all these people?'

He replied that if I didn't return many people would never get the opportunity to hear about his love and saving grace because many of them will never set foot inside a church.

Knowing I was a child of God now, I ask the Lord to allow me to return. My goal will be to share love and compassion with the ones I meet. Through some mysterious way, that only God knows, I was given the opportunity to see Paradise and to talk with the Lord. I was here in Paradise once and I knew I would come back again. With all my heart I wanted to come back, but only in Gods time.

Before allowing me to return he shared a few things with me. Some I would remember clearly and others, he said, I would remember as I needed to.

'My precious child, you must see things in a new light.'

Through his love I understood that I needed to see through his eyes, the eyes of love and righteousness. Through the eyes of eternity I needed to see the world as God sees it.

Looking into his glorious light I ask, 'How do I return? Do I return the way I came or just how do I get back?'

'Precious child, tilt your head, feel the liquid drain from your eyes. Then open your eyes and see. I had no remembrance of the journey back; all I remember is closing my eyes and waking up in the hospital bed. Instantly I was back in my body with the head of the bed tilted downward. Ever so slowly I opened my eyes. I saw a doctor at the end of the bed with some kind of instrument poking at my feet looking for any sign of life. The doctor did not realize I was alive and looking up at him.

'Lord, he thinks I'm dead. Give him a sign that I am alive.' Almost instantly the Lord answered my prayer and the doctor looked into my eyes. Terror swept over his face and all color had drained from his face, which left him as white as a sheet. 'She's alive, she's alive, he screamed.

With what strength I had I looked towards the hallway and seen nurses, orderlies, family members and other doctors staring at me in disbelief and astonishment. Later that day it was explained to me why they had looked at me the way they did. I was clinically dead and had no vital signs. They could not find a sign of life. I was in the thrones of death for thirty minutes, they thought. I am forever grateful that the doctors did not give up on me.

I felt weak from the ordeal and closed my eyes but immediately opened them again to be sure I was alive and in my body. An eerie feeling came over me to whether or not I would disappear again. Once I was sure that indeed I was alive, I fell into a peaceful sleep and did not awaken until the next day. As I opened my eyes I saw my pastor sitting by the bed holding my hand, praying. The realization that I was alive brought a 'hallelujah' from his lips. Hearing the commotion the doctors and nurses entered my room.

'Rough night?' my pastor asks.

'Yeah, one I will never forget.'

It is my belief that the doctors had told him of the overdose but still, in his eyes, there was love and compassion for me. He knew that it was possible that he would have a funeral service to perform. I did not know it at the time but he had been with me the whole night through.

The doctor examined me thoroughly and said I could go home. Most of the drugs had worn off but still there was a still some effects I would have to deal with. Dizziness was one of the effects, so as soon as I got home I went to bed. Exhaustion and hunger enveloped my body but I was too weak to get up and eat so again I fell asleep. Suddenly in the middle of the night I woke up in a cold, wet shiver. Terror filled my heart as there were monsters before me. Eight to ten pair of them with red glowing eyes, slit like a cat, instead of round eyes. Their bodies were half human and half animal.

What are they?

Looking into my eyes, they leered and snarled that they had come back to get me. The one closest to me snarled that they had come back to get me and take me back.

'No, I am not coming back.' I screamed.

Am I going insane? Am I going to mentally snap? I had done through so much in the last couple of days.

Settling down was my main priority. Laying there I cried out to the Lord and ask him what was going on. Slowly and methodically he took me through everything I had gone through. This series of events were seared into my mind.

'Lord, why do these creatures want to attack me?'

Holly Jo, do you remember the Lord's Prayer?

I tried to remember even a portion of the prayer but couldn't.

Finally, the words came to me and I prayed the Lord's Prayer through releasing me from the evil ones. With my whole heart and soul I prayed the prayer over and over.

'Turn the lights off, my child.' Nothing happened. The Lord's Prayer had been effective and I went back to sleep.

The next morning as I was preparing breakfast some well meaning friends stopped by. They began talking but it was like they were talking in a different language, for nothing they said had any meaning. It was very confusing as if I was hearing two different messages. The veil that had covered me was now lifted and I could see through their masks. In the new light that the Lord had granted to me, I began to see things differently for the first time in my life. The intents of their hearts were totally contrary to what they were speaking. I was really frightened because I did not know how to react to that kind of understanding. So I excused myself, withdrew to the bedroom and stayed there.

After the events of the night before, I thought there would be no more, but I sure was mistaken. Later during the night I awoke in a cold sweat because there was something nearby that scared me.

Slightly turning my head I saw that the demon monsters had returned. Yet for some reason they couldn't get to me, even though they were intimidating me. Within my heart there was a deep peace and I knew, beyond a shadow of a doubt, that I had seen the light of God and that this light was within me. I knew no matter how small this light was, it was within me and the demons could not come in. The Bible says once a demon returns he brings seven worse than himself. These demons wanted me back in the worst way and were doing their best to terrify me into coming back.

With such a sudden movement, that startled the demons, I leapt from my bed and knelt there. There was a battle raging around me as I pled the blood of Jesus over me. I recited the Lord's Prayer over and over again until there was peace within. After I felt this peace I returned to bed and fell asleep.

As I awoke the next morning the peace remained. Later on that morning a man knocked on my door. Recognizing the man I opened the door but the moment I saw his eyes I knew he was one of the demons, the same red tinge I had seen in all the other demons and monsters that had haunted me the last two nights. His voice bellowed that tonight I was coming with them and they were going to take me somewhere. To back this statement up he called on others to join him. With all the strength I could muster, I tried to push the door shut but this man had gained a supernatural strength and I couldn't budge the door.

'In the name of Jesus—go!' I screamed at them.

As if he had been punched in the chest this man reeled back. As he recoiled I slammed the door and locked it. For the meantime I was safe.

The next day was peaceful until that evening when this same man was back throwing stones at my window. The doors were secured and they were locked, but inadvertently I had left a small window open.

Whatever these demons were they were out to kill me using humans for that purpose.

Realizing the window was open I went to close it but a big hand came through and released the latch.

'Come out, Holly Jo.' I pretended I didn't hear the voice but the pelting of the stones were getting louder.

'Holly Jo,' a voice shouted loudly, 'Come out.' This voice sounded like a female and she was becoming angrier and angrier. The stones, which were being pelted against the window, became heavier. Then suddenly a spear came flying through the window.

Okay, the best form of defense is attack, so I reached for the flashlight that I kept by my bed and flashed it into the spear wielders eyes and seen the same red tint as I had seen before. Screaming, I grabbed the spear and threw it back at whoever was the closest. Before they had a chance of attack again I slammed the window shut.

I shined the flashlight outside and could see two women and two men cowering away like frightened animals about to be stoned. It really amazed me how afraid of the light they were.

Holly Jo, you are a Christian and as such you have the power of God within you.

Notwithstanding, the demons had yet another attack in store for me. I was awakened in the middle of the night being violently shaken. I knew how to get rid of them by reciting the Lord's Prayer and using the name of Jesus. They had to go. I was so furious that I decided to verbally give them a lashing.

Sitting on the edge of the bed I said, 'I am sick of these demons harassing me in the middle of the night. What must I do to get rid of them?'

The answer came clear and sharp. *Read your Bible!!!* I immediately jumped up, rushed to the living room and grabbed my Bible and started reading from the beginning. In the beginning God created the heavens and earth. The earth was an empty, formless mass cloaked in darkness. Hovering over it was the Spirit of God. Let there be light. Genesis 1:3. God saw it was good. Then he separated the light from the darkness. He called the light—day and the darkness—night. Genesis 1: 4.

Lord Jesus, I have been so proud. Pride goeth before a fall. Forgive me!!

Since these experiences with the demons I have been following Jesus Christ as my personal Savior and he has given me the desire of my heart, which is to be a well known author. (Not quite there, but will be).

I am indebted to Jesus, beyond measure, for what he has done for me and to be faithful and true to him is my only desire.

I find great satisfaction in living for Christ and being a witness to His healing and saving power.

Hebrews 13 5, 6 and 8: "For he hath said, I will never leave thee nor forsake thee. So that we may boldly say, The Lord is my helper and I will not fear what man shall do unto me. Jesus Christ the same yesterday, today and forever."

CHAPTER 2

EPRESSION HAD ME IN its grip and I felt that life was no longer worth living, so with suicide in mind I downed a bottle of medication, hoping it would release me from my misery. My breathing became labored and soon after all breathing stopped. As far as the world was concerned I was dead, but in another world I was alive. I now found myself outside my body floating. 'I'm dead, I'm dead!!'

After a second or two a sense of peace overcame all my emotions and I was looking at my life—less my body, but I did not care. To me it was a relief it was over.

I drifted upward through the ceiling and into an extremely peaceful darkness. From inside this darkness I heard the most awesome humming and singing sounds. I floated listening to the vibrant richness of the sound, while at the same time moving slowly toward a speck of light that grew bigger and bigger as I neared.

The dazzling, sparkling light begins to drive away this pleasing darkness that was in hues never seen. I found this light emitting from an individual wearing a pure, white robe. I now was standing in front of him. Like a heavy sack of wheat, I fell and wept at his feet. With a hand so gentle, he touched my shoulder and told me to stand.

Looking into this astonishing person's eyes I seen my life's course shown to me, which revealed I was without excuse. At that moment I knew I was being judged and deserved punishment. For now all I could do is stand directly in front of him, his hood covering his face and receive my sentence. As I stood looking at him I saw physical wounds on his hands and feet. His forehead bore scars from the crown of thorns and his wrists showed deeply cut gashes. By bearing the great weight of the world, his bones clearly showed every joint had been ripped apart. Seeing his great love, I stood there ashamed.

He spoke, but not orally. This was hard for me to understand but still I heard every word he spoke, as if he was speaking aloud.

His words to me were that I was to experience heaven and hell. With that said I was whirled through time and space and found myself on the shore line of a great ocean of fire. Standing on the shore I recognized people, I knew, who were in the lake of fire. This was hard for me to understand because I thought some of them were Christians.

Revelation 21: 8: "The Lake that burneth with fire and brimstone."

Let me say a few things about hell. First of all it is a place of constant torment, uncontrolled hurt and someone having power over you. All who do evil will have a place in the lake of fire and brimstone. The smoke from their burning pain will rise forever and ever. This will be the second death.

This lake will be filled with flames with people burning inside the flames. They will be crying and screaming—they will burn but will never be consumed. I know this to be a fact because I was there because of my foolishness in trying to take my own life.

'Go back, go back, don't come to this place, there is no way out, *no escape* if you come here. I repeat 'no way out.'

In the eyes of these people there was such agony and pain, but the most painful thing was their loneliness. Depression, here, was extremely prevalent because these people knew they had no hope, no escape from this place of horrors. The stench was worse than anything I had ever smelt, terrible and extremely nauseating. It reminded me of sulfur.

Growing up my life had been full of extreme abuse. I had experienced beatings, was raped, sodomized and abused in many other ways, but what I was seeing here scared me to death, because I did not understand it. I starred in the lake of fire, heard the screams and seen the tortures and I became entrapped in the darkness. When I awoke my body and spirit had rejoined and I was lying in a hospital bed.

After being released from the hospital I was sent home thinking this bad experience was behind me, but, oh, how wrong I was.

In the middle of the night I awoke hearing voices. In a sweet tone they were coaxing me to come with them quickly. 'Come quickly with us, we have been waiting for you.' Suddenly I was surrounded by people who were moving me on. The farther we went the darker it became. The demeanors of these people were now becoming more and more impatient and openly hostile to me. They were using syrupy sweet words in order for me to follow them. Now that I was in their grasp they shouted, hurry up, keep moving, shut up, and stop asking questions. These words were followed with extreme profanity and things had gotten ugly.

I am absolutely afraid of the dark but here I was in complete and total darkness. Darkness—total darkness. The darkness was pressing, not only did the darkness exist beyond but it existed within. The hostility of these people was worse than ever.

I stopped and told them I wasn't going any farther because I did not know where I was going. 'You're almost there.' They replied.

I started fighting and trying to get away from them, but they pushed, pulled and shoved me. They were furious because I was trying to get away. When they had come to me in the hospital room there were only a handful of them but now it seemed like there were thousands of them.

These people were playing with me and could have destroyed me if they wanted to, but they didn't want to.

Because these people derived satisfaction from the pain I experienced they continually inflicted pain upon me. Tearing, biting, ripping, gouging and scratching with their fingernails were one of the tortures. Defending myself, trying to fight them off was a losing battle, for there were thousands all over me.

All ripped up and suffering excruciating pain over my entire body, inside and out, I found myself lying on the ground. The emotional pain with utter degradation was harder to bear than the physical pain. Was it unjust or wrong? That I couldn't tell.

Distinctly I heard a voice say **Pray to God.** I hadn't prayed in many years but I tried to remember a prayer from childhood. Into my mind came the Lord's Prayer. I tried to pray it but the words became jumbled up and I became confused. This confusion was causing me to forget the prayers I had learned as a child. I thought even if I could pray, I didn't know how anymore.

Every time the word God was spoken it was like pouring boiling water on these people. They would yell, scream and shriek and the worst profanity I had ever heard spilled from their mouths. They could not bear the name of Jesus. When I used the name of Jesus I could see it was very painful for them and they would back away every time I spoke the name of Jesus. Talking about and using the name of Jesus gave me a sense I could push them away.

The name of Jesus caused these people to leave and I found myself alone. Alone to think of the things I had done and also of the things I hadn't done in my life.

One conclusion I came to was that my only god was myself and that through my entire life I had been selfish and self-centered.

Suddenly a realization came to me, that there was something terribly wrong in my life and that these people who attacked me were the same kind of a person as I was. Monsters or demons they were not but were people who had missed *IT*. They missed the point of being alive in the world. Selfishness and cruelty were their way of life. Now I found myself in the same world where there was nothing but selfishness and cruelty. Without end they were doomed to inflict that upon each other and themselves, without end and the worst part was I had become a part of it.

Because of the way I lived my thought was I deserved to be here, even though I didn't want to be.

There is no way you can imagine how emotionally painful that was.

When I was young and innocent I believed in something good, someone other than myself. I wanted back the person who was good, all powerful and who really cared about me.

The things I had lost, thrown away, I wanted back. I didn't know Jesus, but my heart ached to know him. I didn't know his love, but I wanted to. I didn't know if he was real but, oh, how I wanted him to be real.

"God, if you exist and Jesus if you are God's Lamb please kill me or cure me. I don't want to live anymore. I am a worthless, selfish, no-good person." Instantly after crying out, the darkness and blackness left my life. The guilt I carried left my life, the violence, anger and hatred also left my life. Jesus Christ became my Lord and Savior. I believe Jesus is the Son of God and that he saved my soul. Keep me alive. When I die keep me out of the burning pits of hell.

God healed my mind, my memory and took away my desire to self-mutilate myself and took away the desire of overdosing on pills. All this was instantaneously gone and I was delivered.

At one time in my life I believed in something and I wanted to trust that was true.

Lying there in the darkness I looked up and said' Jesus, save me' and he came. Into the darkness came a very small speck of light and then swiftly it became brighter. If I had been in the physical world this light would have consumed me and burnt me to a crisp. But here in the spiritual world it was not hot or dangerous. Through this light Jesus reached down and gently picked me up.

In this world all my gory, filthy would could be seen. Road kill looked better than I did. He gently put his hand underneath me and with tenderness and compassion picked me up into his arms. The dirt, pain and the wounds disappeared at the touch of his hand. Everything evaporated and was healed and made whole. My heart was filled with Jesus' love. If I were to live to be a thousand years old I could never explain fully the love of God. I become frustrated because I am not able to explain to people the depths of God's love because it is the best thing that ever happened in my life.

As Jesus holds me in his arms, he is ever so gently rubbing my back. I had never felt such love. I cried and cried because of the happiness I felt because I was lost but now am found. I was dead but was brought back to life. Holding me gently and securely we flew out of the place of darkness.

As we moved towards the light a tremendous thought of shame filled my heart. Throughout my life I had done nothing good, mostly bad things. I thought of myself as dirt, garbage and filth. A thought came to me that God had made a mistake and that I didn't belong here with him and that he didn't want me. How could such a loving God want a sinner like me, who had done nothing but bad in her life?

My thoughts were known to him as if I had spoken them aloud. Without a moment's notice he stopped somewhere between heaven and hell. He stood me up in front of him and looking me squarely in the eyes said; 'My most precious child, I do not make mistakes, you belong here.' While we were stopped he revealed many things to me. Some I would remember when the time came.

While we were in this suspended area God called some angels to our spot and instructed them to show me my life from conception to the present time. For me, looking back over my past was very difficult to do. During this look back the angels showed me the things I had done right and the bad things I had done. In simplicity it was spelled out. I was shown the times when I had been loving, kind and considerate which made the angels happy and in turn had pleased Jesus. Also it pleased God, the Father. But the times in my life when I had been selfish and manipulative grieved the angel's heart. Also the heart of Jesus was hurt by my actions. Of course, God, the Father was hurt also. What the angels were trying to convey to me, in a nutshell, was that the whole purpose of my existence was to love God and to love my neighbors as myself. The reason I was created was to do and learn, but I had failed miserably. After they had explained to me the things I needed to know they told me that I needed to return to earth. I wanted to continue on the journey to heaven so this remark really saddened me. The angels assured me that heaven was a fun, interesting and wonderful place. 'You are not ready and it is not your time to go to heaven. It is time for you to return to earth and live the way God wants you to, the way he created you to live.'

I felt I could not live in the world without them that my heart would break if I went back. They would be in heaven and I would be earthbound. One of the angels said to me; 'You don't get it. What's the matter? We are showing you all this and we have been with you always. All the time we have been with you and never once have you been alone.'

'Okay, but you have to let me know you are around once in awhile.' I replied to them.

The angels explained to me that I needed to pray and confess my sins to God and give him all my worries, cares, hopes and dreams. Totally give them all up to God. I knew than that there would be times that I would know, in my heart, that they were there. I may not necessarily see them, but I would feel their presence.

'If you can assure me that there will be times when I know that love, then I feel I can live in the world.'

The angels assured me they would and then I was sent back to earth. There is a reason that each and every one of us are on earth and each of us has important lessons to learn in life. One lesson we must learn is that heaven is real but so is hell. Heaven is a place you want to go and hell is a place you want to miss.

CHAPTER 3

FTER A LONG EXHAUSTING day I felt tired and was having chest pains. I knew I must relax so I laid down hoping the pain would subside. It didn't, only got worse. Suddenly I felt my soul leaving my body. I floated upward leaving my physical body lying in the bed. Through the darkness I seen a great iron gate, I entered. On the other side I seen no one nor did I hear any noise. I moved away from the doorway and begin walking straight ahead. After I had walked quite a distance I came to the banks of a broad river. Here it was semi-light. Before long I heard a splashing sound of someone rowing a boat. The boat stopped beside the shore and the man told me to get in, that I was to go with him. Not another word was spoken as he rowed across the river. Reaching the other side I got out, as instructed to, and before my eyes the boatman disappeared.

I stood there dazed and confused, not knowing what to do. Looking around I noticed two roads leading through a dark valley. The broad one seemed well-traveled, whereas the narrow road was less traveled. Of course, I took the well-traveled road. Before long total darkness enveloped me and the only thing that guided me was a speck of light that would flicker in a distance.

As I came to the end of the road I was met by a hideous creature, that to describe him would be utterly impossible, but I will try and give you a faint hint of his hideous appearance. He resembled a man, but was much larger than any man I had ever seen. My guess would be that he was at least 10 feet or over, for he towered greatly over me. I had to crank my head backwards and look up in order to see his face. There were giant wings on his back; he was nude and black as coal. In his hand he held a spear which appeared to be fifteen feet in length. His eyes shone like balls of fire, his teeth were pure white and looked like fangs, his nose was broad and flat, like something had smashed it in, and his hair was coarser than horse's hair and this hair hung down to his shoulders. His voice sounded like the growl of a lion.

My body trembled as I saw the glimmer of the spear pointing my way, thinking he was going to plunge it through my heart. But instead he told me to follow him that he would be my guide on this journey. I followed. After walking for a considerable time we came to a gigantic wall with a huge door. Over the door these words tore at my soul. *'THIS IS HELL;'* and every letter was capitalized.

With his spear he gave three distinctive raps and the door opened. Through the darkness I was conducted down a long hallway by the sound of my guide's heavy footsteps. Along the way I heard moans as if someone was dying. The farther we went the intensity of the moaning increased. I heard them screaming, 'Water, Water.' Through another door the cry for water became more thunderous with millions and millions crying out for water.

We entered through another door and beyond this door was a wide open plain.

My first guide had vanished and another hideous creature took his place. He held a spear, as the first one had. His voice struck horror to my soul as he told me that he had come to tell me of my future doom.

'You are in hell and all hope for you is gone. Did you hear the moaning of the lost souls crying out for water to cool their parched tongues? Along the hallway did you notice a door off to the side? Well, that is the door that opens to the lake of fire and this is to be your doom. Before a guide takes you to this place of torment; from whence there is no hope for those who enter there. You will be permitted to stay in the open plain, for a short time, where it is granted to all the lost souls to look upon what they could have enjoyed, instead of what they must suffer now.'

The creature disappeared instantly and I was alone and petrified. I collapsed to the ground in a helpless mass as the strength in my legs evaporated and weakness took hold of my body and all strength left me. Drowsiness suddenly overtook me—I was neither asleep nor awake, but I begin dreaming. Off in a far distance I could see the beautiful city that is mentioned in the Bible. The beautiful city of Jerusalem. It shone with the glory of God and was as bright as diamonds. The foundations of the city were decorated with every kind of jewels. The first foundation was Jasper—second—Sapphire, third—Chalcedony, fourth—Emerald, fifth—Onyx, sixth—Carnelian, seventh—Chrysolyte, eighth—Beryl, ninth—Topaz, tenth—Chrysoprasus, eleventh—Jacinth and the twelfth—Amethyst. Revelation 21:19-20. Every wall of jasper was remarkably beautiful and every way I looked were vast plains of beautiful flowers spanning out. I beheld the river of life which was as clear as crystal and the city was pure gold like unto clear glass. Revelation 21:18. Coming from the multitudes was beautiful, melodious music. They sang as they passed in and out through the gates of the city.

Before me stood my dear sister. Her prayer before she died was that I would accept Christ as my Savior but her prayer had gone unanswered. I know her heart was broken. Looking at me she beckoned for me to come to her but I couldn't move. It was as if a heavy weight was holding me down. As a gentle breeze blew it floated the fragrance of the flowers towards me and now I could clearly hear the sweet music of angel's voice. This fragrance released me from the heaviness and soon I was embracing my sister.

Oh! That I could be one of them, I mumbled to myself.

This wonderful bliss was suddenly dashed away from me and I was awakened from my slumber. An inmate of my dark abode awakened me from my happy dreamland. This inmate told me it was now time to enter my future doom. I followed him retracing my steps through the dark hallway. Finally we stopped and in front of us was the doorway to the lake of fire. As far as my eyes could see the lake was filled with fire and brimstone. Huge waves, of fire, rolled over each other and great waves leapt high in the air, like waves during a violent storm. These storms would envelope people and roll them over and over. People would rise on the crest of waves, then be carried away to the depths of this dreadful lake of fire. As the people rose upon the crest their curses against God were horrifying and their pitiful wails for water were heart wrenching. Echoing and re-echoing in this region were the laments of these lost souls.

Written upon this door were these words. *This is your doom—Eternity never ends.* The door was opened and I was told to enter. As I entered my legs gave way and I found myself sinking into the lake of fire with an indescribable thirst for water seizing me. As I cried for water I awoke in my bed.

I know there is a heaven and hell, *an old-fashioned hell* that the Bible tells us about.

On thing is certain—I am never going to that place ever again.

I am going to live and die a Christian.

The horrifying sights of hell will never leave my mind, but neither will the beautiful sights of heaven. In heaven I will meet my loved ones. Beside the beautiful river I will sit down on its banks, reveling in the beauty of it all. I'll move here and there with angels as we walk across the plains, though the valley and over the hills carpeted with sweet smelling flowers. The beauty of it all far surpassed anything mortal could imagine. As we walked I listened to the songs of the saved.

CHAPTER 4

OD HELP ME!!! GOD Help Me!!!

I was raised in a church which didn't seem to satisfy the hunger in my soul. So as I grew older I drifted away from church. The devil had me convinced that no one cared, so I descended into prescription drug abuse and other over the counter drugs. I did this to relieve the feeling of not being wanted. Deep down inside, I hoped and prayed I would not wake up. But through it all I survived.

I had only been married a short time when the enemy attacked me with full force. It was the demon was saying 'You're mine, you're mine and this time I will have you.' A friend, who had been staying at our house, had gotten sick so I volunteered to take her to the hospital. After she had been called into the examination room, I felt the enemy grab hold of me and led me to the gift shop where I bought a bottle of sleeping pills and a coke. I went back to the emergency waiting room and took the bottle of pills. Once the enemy has a hold of you, your life is not yours and you are in his power.

All the time I had spent in church there never once was anything said about how to resist the attacks of the enemy. It is my belief that is the reason I could not stop myself from doing the things I did.

The sleeping pills worked rapidly and within a short time I was unconscious. I remember thinking of a song before blackness took over. *"He Lives, he lives, Christ Jesus lives today. He walks with me and talks with me along life's narrow way. He lives, he lives, Salvation to impart. You ask me how I know he lives; he lives within my heart."*

It wasn't long before a rapid decline in my vitals happened. My heart rate drastically declined, my pulse and blood pressure were almost non-existent. The next morning, as I started to regain consciousness, I remember a doctor standing over me and to me he looked like he had crossed eyes. He was not very pleasant and almost immediately after I became awake he told the nurses to release me. No concern, no compassion-no questions on why-only get her out of here.

If God hadn't forgiven me that night I don't think anyone else would have. Through my life I always felt like I was the black sheep of the family even though there were several other children.

Jeremiah 29: 13 says, "And ye shall seek me and find me, when ye shall search for me with all your heart."

While I was unconscious I was thrown into outer darkness into the wailing and gnashing of teeth. I had never heard such tormenting, horrifying screams in my life. Their screams were so loud I believe they could have broken the sound barrier. Screams escaped from my mouth as I heard theirs.

I thought my head would burst open from so many demons screaming. For you non-believers that don't think there are demons you are wrong beyond belief. There are demons of every shape, and size, every color and from every ethnic group. Beware they are everywhere!!! These demons will fool you into believing that what they say is true. Then these demons, which appear before you, at first as beautiful, trustworthy creatures will turn into hideous creatures once they have you in their grasp. There will be unbelievable profanity and cursing. They will begin snarling that they have you and that there is no way you will escape. They will admit they fooled you in order to get you within their grasp. *So Beware!!!*

To prove their point, that I deserved to be in hell, they showed me the sins I had committed in my life. Disobedience to my parents, stealing, lying and many more bad things I had done. As my sins were brought before me a scream escaped from my lips.

Later I would be asked how long I thought I had spent in hell. My reply was that I didn't know but that it seemed like an eternity. All I know is that the nightmare lasted all night long.

I can tell you one thing ***I do not want to go back!!!***

Just before I awoke I was shown the lake of fire, but this time with God by my side. In this lake of fire millions and millions of people burnt within the unquenchable fire. Their bodies were whole and were never consumed and their screams were terrifying and ear-deafening. This scene was a scary thing to see but God laid his hand gently on my shoulder and I felt at peace, knowing as long as he was by my side I would be protected. Thousands of people were on the brink of the lake falling as waves would consume them. God told me that I was going to pull them out of hell and that people would be saved by my testimony before they fell into the lake of fire.

By the grace of God these demons can be cast out. Demons are truly afraid of Christians because Christ abides within us. God is everywhere, in heaven, on earth and, yes, even in hell.

I am a sinner saved by grace. Ephesians 2: 8: "For by grace are ye saved through faith . . ."

I was once lost but now am found.

There is a God who can take away every pain, disease, heartaches and he can restore your memory.

CHAPTER 5

$\mathcal{M}$Y MIND AND SPIRIT were fully alert as I faded away. Chaos and abuse were a way of living for me and I thought the only way to escape was through death. Suddenly a powerful storm, like a tornado flattened the landscape where I was until there were no trees or anything else standing, only a flat barren plain. Alone and with no one else I hurried across the plain as fast as I could. In the midst of this plain was a river I had to cross, which was as black as coal and slimy. As I reached the other side I saw a terrible, terrible lake which was glowing with fire. Everything here was intensified a hundred times, the water, the smell, what I heard, saw and touched. The smell was pungent like rotting garbage and the decay of flesh. I was confused until I seen Satan. His face and body was like a lion but his legs were like a serpent spirit. A number of horns protruded from his head and I was petrified by his appearance. I stood there trembling but finally got the nerve to ask him who he was. He said he was the destroyer; the King of Hell. He instructed me to look into the lake, the lake burning with brimstone. Revelation 19: 20. Here I seen friends whom I thought were good Christians. One in particular was an evangelist whom I thought was very much in tune with God. He traveled far and wide preaching the word of God. Why would such a godly man be here in the lake of fire? Only God knew the reason. Maybe he had done things in his life that were not pleasing to God and never ask the Lord to forgive him for these things.

Another person I seen was a pastor. Her life was godly on Sunday; she preached and taught God's word but the rest of the time she was doing her own thing. That is why she was here in the lake of fire. There was another woman who professed to be a Christian but yet treated people unfairly and with malice. It was either her way or none at all. I could see the reason why she was here.

I was instructed to look at another person. This person's face was filled with hatred. Who is this man and why is his face so full of hatred. I then remembered that he was the one who had killed millions and millions of people. His murderous ways were the reason he was here.

Another look into the lake and I seen a giant of a man, who was three times taller than anyone else. This man was Goliath. The reason he was here was because he blasphemed against the eternal God and God's servant David. The story of David and Goliath is recorded in 1 Samuel 17.

These people and hordes of others were screaming and lamenting in their torment and pain.

Moving closer to the shore I seen thousands upon thousands more people being sent to this place of torment and pain. Their gender I could distinguish but their faces I could not recognize.

I looked away from the shore and seen there were walls and these walls bore entrances to different caves. These walls extended far beyond my sight. The beach was covered with people being laid out.

Choosing one of these entrances I started walking down its path. On either side were people attached to the walls and as I walked they called out to me and tried to grab me. My best chance would be to stay in the middle, never swaying to the left or to the right for fear I would be seized immediately. As I came to an opening there was a ledge that went straight across. My heart pounded as I walked on the ledge, so I walked very carefully because I did not want to fall. About half-way across I was feeling pretty sure of myself and felt I could make it all the way across. Guess, I had too much assurance in myself and I lost my footing and fell. Hanging there I looked down and to my horror there was a demon face as large as a round table. This face was carved out of the rock and it dripped with water and mud. This place was dank and gloomy. With all the strength within me I pulled myself back upon the ledge, caught my breath and safely made it to the other side, but I was not free from experiencing more of hell. Once I stepped foot off the ledge I was led to a different section of hell. Here the rich and poor were preparing their evening meal.

I turned to the King of hell and ask who prepared the meals. He told me that the poor prepare their own meals and the rich have someone prepare it for them. The moment the rich start eating a smoke surrounds them causing them to eat fast, trying to ease their consciences. The reason for the fast eating is that they were fearful of losing their money. Their money was their god.

There was a creature whose job it was to stroke the fires beneath the lake, keeping it very hot. This creature asks me if I was going into the lake of fire.

'No, I am just here to observe.'

This creature, stroking the fire, was terrifying. Upon his head were ten horns and in his hand was a spear that had seven sharp blades coming from its end. This creature looked me in the eyes and said; 'You are right, you are just an observer. I cannot find your name here, so you must now go back the way you came.' With this he pointed me towards the desolate plains. Upon arriving back on the desolate plains, I seen no one, so I walked and walked, soon my feet were bleeding and in great pain for these plains were extremely hot. At long last I came to a cross roads, one road was wide and went off to the left and the other much smaller road went off to the right. Upon a signpost were written these words; 'The wide road is for those who not believe in the Lord Jesus Christ and the smaller road is for believers in Christ.'

I was curious so I started down the wide road and in the distance I seen a couple people. My desire was to catch up with them so we could walk together, but no matter how hard I tried I couldn't catch up with them. I made my way back to the fork in the road and as I stood there watching the two figures continue down the road, I suddenly heard blood curdling screams, for these two figures were killed, by stabbing, at the end of the road. Seeing what had happened to them I let out a gasp of relieve. The smaller road which I now traveled led me to another road, which was paved in pure gold and was so shiny I could see my reflection. As I walked a man in a pure white robe appeared before me. I heard the most glorious music cascading behind him.

'Come and walk with me,' he said. As we walked I ask him his name but he did not answer. After walking for quite some time he stopped and looking into my face said, 'I am the one who holds the keys to heaven. Heaven is a beautiful, gorgeous place, but you will not be able to go there now, but if you follow Jesus Christ you will be able to enter heavens gates after your life on earth is finished.' Finally he told me his name was Peter.

Peter said to me, 'Sit down and look to the north and see how God created man.' In a distance I saw the eternal God. He spoke to an angel saying, 'Let us make man.' Genesis 1: 26. The angel replied and pleaded with God, 'Please don't make man, for he will wrong and grieve you.' But God made man anyway. God created man from the dust of the earth and blew in the nostrils of man and man came to life. God called him Adam. Genesis 2: 7.

I was told by Peter to get up and go back to where I came from. Speak to the people who worship idols (idols are anything you put before God). Tell them they will go to hell if they do not change their ways. All those who do not believe in the Lord Jesus Christ will go to hell. Go back to earth and testify of the things you have seen. Many will come to know the Lord Jesus Christ through your testimony.

There was no way I wanted to go back to earth; I wanted to go on to heaven. Appearing before me was an angel and she held a book in her hands. She opened it looking for my name. first she looked for my childhood name, no luck, then she looked for my nickname, which my brother had given me, again no luck, then she looked for my given name, but it wasn't there wither. Your name is not written in this book so you must return to earth and testify to all around of the love and peace of God.

"Do not be afraid of what others say because if God is for us who can be against us." Romans 8: 31.

As I turned to start my way back to earth, I ask Peter if he would walk with me. He graciously said he would. As we traveled this road melodious, heavenly, sweet and beautiful music followed us. My walk with Peter along the road was a joyous one, for we talked of many things. We finally came to a spot where I would return to earth. Here there were ladders that reached from the heaven to the sky, not reaching the earth but stopping in mid-air. These ladders were filled with angels, some going up to heaven and others descending down the ladder.

I ask Peter who they were.

He told me they were messengers of God and were reporting to heaven the names of all those who believed in Jesus Christ and the names of those who didn't. 'Now it is time for you to return.'

CHAPTER 6

NOTHER EXPERIENCE.

I was standing near a shore line of a great ocean of fire. How I got there I don't know. One minute I closed my eyes and the next I was standing on this shore line. Revelation 21: 8 tells us, ". . . the lake that burneth with fire and brimstone." This awesome sight of the final judgment was opened to my eyes, which no one was usually allowed to see.

From some distance I stood looking at this burning, violent mass of blue fire. This lake of fire and brimstone was the same as far as the eye could see. Presently there was no one in it, but there were people on the shore that I had known in life. My mother, who died of a heart attack, my father, who died from cirrhosis of the liver, my mother and father-in law, both dying from heart trouble, my grandfather, who I believed had been murdered, my sister, who had died from cancer and so many more. We all knew each other but didn't speak. Standing there we were perplexed and in deep thought as though we could not believe what we were seeing. Every face showed bewilderment and confusion. There were no words to explain, except to say we were eyewitnesses to the final judgment.

No escape—no way out.

There was no escaping this prison except by divine intervention.

In an audible voice I said, "If only I had known about this place I would have done anything required, of me, to escape coming here to a place like this." But alas, I had not known.

Almost instantly a man appeared in front of me and I knew immediately who he was. He had a kind, strong, compassionate face, composed and unafraid. Master of all, Jesus himself.

Taking hold of me was great hope, knowing the answer to my problem was this great and wonderful person that was moving towards me in this prison of lost confused judgment bound souls. I had done nothing to attract his attention but I thought to myself: "If only he would look my way and see me, he would rescue me from this place because he would know I had never been taught what hell was like." I knew deep down inside he would know what to do. But instead of looking at me as he passed on by, which shattered my thoughts of getting out of here. BUT!! Just before passing out of sight he looked directly at me and that is all it took and that was enough.

In a split second I was back and entering my body. Suddenly life was restored and I came back into my body and I opened my eyes.

Beyond a shadow of a doubt I know there is a *Lake of fire,* for I have seen and experienced it. I know Jesus is alive in eternity.

Revelation 1: 9-11 states; "I, John . . . was in the spirit on the Lords day and heard behind me a great voice, as a trumpet, saying, I am Alpha and Omega, the beginning and the end."

As I lay in the hospital bed I was in constant communication with the Holy Spirit. I thought about my life, the things I had seen with my out-of-body experience, such as the lake of fire. Seeing the lake of fire frightened me more than anything I had ever seen. I thought of the many friends and relatives I had seen while in hell. Another thing I thought about was coming back. I knew God's spirit would be with me continually. I ask the Holy Spirit to untangle my twisted philosophy until I could understand what was happening to me, now. The Holy Spirit showed me what had been wrong in my past, my many sins, and my promiscuous ways and then he helped me piece it all together until it made sense why this had happened to me.

Right then and there, on my hospital bed, I prayed that God would show me his will and the things he wanted me to do.

Speaking to God I told him that I would do my best in whatever he wanted me to do.

Through all this I have learned that you have to be very, very positive in your stand against negative suggestions that come to dishearten our faith in trials and tribulations. These difficult times are sent to make us stronger, so that we may be able to stand against the devil.

Ephesians 6: 11 says, "Put on the whole armour of God that ye may be able to stand against the wiles of the devil."

Another verse that tells us that we must, submit ourselves to God is found in James 4: 7, "Submit yourselves therefore to God. Resist the devil and he will flee from you."

Our natural minds rob us of supernatural victory.

Believe God and act whether you understand or not.

CHAPTER 7

As I lay supine upon my bed I felt my soul leaving my body. It was like a breath of fresh air had enveloped me and I rose higher and higher, leaving my earthly body behind. I came to a stop in front of a man glimmering with a wondrous, heavenly light. There was no way I could have looked into his light if I hadn't been in the spiritual realm. This man spoke to me with such love, calling me his child. We spoke for quite some time and then he told me that at an appointed time I was to see another land. After I got to this other land I was to speak the name of Jesus and see what I would see. He told me it was arranged beforehand once for a person to die.

Hebrews 9: 27: ". . . everyone must die once . . ."

It was an option of the Father if we were to return.

Just before pointing to a tunnel he told me I would return the same way I came. After he spoke these words a gentle breeze lifted me up, feet first, as he did so I noticed I was wearing a robe. As I entered the tunnel I was swallowed up in a violent vortex heading toward a shaft of yellow light. I fell with a thud on the ground as I came to the end of the tunnel. Gathering my bearings I stood up and looked around. There on a hill I noticed a house and a horrendous smelling odor emitted from this house. Also my ears were picking up strange sounds. With joyful shouts people emerged from the house to welcome me.

'Where am I?

'Heaven or hell.'

'Is this paradise?'

'No, it can't be the smells and sounds are wrong.'

From these people something eerie emitted for they appeared translucent. It dawned on me who these people really were—strange foul creatures giving off the illusion of people from the depths of hell. Two words erupted from my mouth; *"Jesus Christ."* These words continually flowed from my mouth until I was free from these creatures.

Complete terror filled me as I realized where I was.

A creature appeared before me and told me to follow him. I obeyed his command because I felt I had no choice. This creature led me to the other side of the horizon where there was a barren land wide, filthy and flat. There were miseries of every kind. An entity traveled with the creature and I. we came to the end of a road and before us there was a hellish sight. There were people in cubicles, which were ten by ten. Each of these cubicles was surrounded by smoke tinted, gelatin like walls. I could see into the cubicles but not out of them.

Each and every one of these cubicles had an individual trapped and unable to escape. Snakes were all over to frighten and intimidate the people there. If that weren't enough there were vicious beast that looked like reptiles patrolling the area. Hell is described in Ezekiel 32: 17-32 as a circular burial pit where the dead are buried within the walls of a pit in accordance to his or her deeds. As you read farther in chapter 32 verses 24-25 it goes on to explain that each individual is placed in a chamber symbolically described as a bed chamber where residents restlessly rest experiencing recompense for his or her deeds performed on earth. (See Ezekiel 32: 30).

In each cubicle people were in various stages of boredom, anguishes and many other torments. Inside these cubicles were ghoulish, evil spirits giving the appearance of people, places and things of each trapped soul acting out scenes from that person's life.

This awful creature, who was guiding me, spoke to me with curses and foul language. As I traveled though this place some of the spirits tried to engage me in conversation. The word *Jesus Christ* flowed, non-stop from my lips because I was terrified.

The hellish tour continued as I observed more lost soul confined to cages. It seemed to me that this journey was lasting forever and I thought it would never end and the more we traveled the more lost souls I seen.

In full measure each person reaped what he/she had sows on earth. Galatians 6: 7: ". . . whatever a man sows, that he will also reap."

Each person trapped in these cages felt a separation from God, knowing they were banished forever and would never know the loving nature of God or true life. Everyone here knew they deserved punishment because they had turned away from God and now lived in this hellish place without God. While these people lived on earth God had in his great justice, fairness and unfathomable love gave them a chance. Now they have what they desired, a place without God.

Many, at first, were deceived that they were in paradise but the real nature of this place was revealed fully to them. Instant anguish was the fate for millions. Hell is truly a place of despair, doom and unending nightmares.

This hideous guide more than once tried to entrap me in one of the cubicles. Fear filled my heart but with the words *Jesus Christ* I was rescued. I found myself being lifter higher and higher until I came before God. Overwhelming me were the sensation of love, mercy, authority, power, justice and righteousness. There was no longer the need to speak the words *Jesus Christ* any longer.

As Jesus held me tight against his bosom I wept profusely onto his robe. No one can enter Heaven except through Jesus Christ.

I now have a renewed comprehension of Gods very deep love, righteousness, justice, mercy and grace.

1 Timothy 1: 15 tells us ". . . that Jesus Christ came into the world to save sinners."

Matthew 18: 11says, "For the Son of man is come to save that which is lost."

Heaven is real.

Hell is real.

Eternity is without end.

Do you want to spend eternity without God?

Death is very final. It takes us away from the ones we need and separates us from the ones we love the most and all that remains is memories.

It's your choice—the decision is yours. Heaven and all its glory or Hell and the torturous burning in the lake of fire.

CHAPTER 8

HIRLING THROUGH A TUNNEL, I came to a sudden stop and there in front of me were these words carved into the gate. "Welcome to Hell." Satan had sent some of his demons to meet me and escort me to a huge waiting room. The waiting room was crowded with people crying pitifully for Jesus to help them. I was shocked by what I seen. No one can say Jesus once, and then live the way they want and then at the end of their lives expect to end up in heaven.

That is a lie.

For Jesus tells us in Matthew 6: 24 that "No man can serve two masters: for either he will hate the one and love the other; or else he will hold on to one and despise the other . . ."

In Luke 16: 13 Jesus reaffirms the. "No servant can serve two masters . . ."

Great fear gripped my soul as I creatures more terrifying than any horror movie. These creatures, or demons, were forcing people forward toward a black passageway. The screams from their pain was deafening. On the side of the passageway was a lake, known as the lake of fire and brimstone.

Revelation 21: 8: ". . . the lake that burneth with fire and brimstone . . ."

The stench was like rotting flesh intermixed with garbage and it took my breath away.

People were thrashing around, in this lake of fire, and cursing because of their pain. Many could be heard crying out to God.

I was so thankful that the Lord was letting me view this scene from a distance. There was no escape for people who were thrown into the lake. Their bodies burned but were never consumed. Satan's demons stood on the shore throwing spears at the ones in the lake and never once did they miss. Each time a spear was thrown, it would hit someone and the cries and screams were deafening from these people who were anguishing. With no end to their pain the people would anguish. Snakes were constantly on guard slithering and crawling around the people frightening them.

Revelation 20: 13: ". . . They were judged, each one according to his works."

Revelation 20: 14: ". . . This is the second death."

Revelation 21: 8: "But the cowardly, unbelieving abominable, murderers, sexually immoral, sorcerers, idolaters and all liars shall have their part in the lake which burns with fire and brimstone, which is the second death."

Once you are in hell there is no time or chance to change.

I discovered a fear in hell that was never on earth. It filled my heart and soul to know there are millions of sleeping Christians on earth.

Wake up!!! It is the last hour.

The Lord is warning us that the days are short and that we need to be ready for his coming.

John 5: 25: ". . . The hour is coming, and now is, when the dead shall hear the voice of the Son of God: and they that hear shall live."

Matthew 24: 36: "But of that day and hour no one knows, not even the angels of heaven, but my Father only."

Believe me, Jesus has the kindest, loving and compassionate eyes, his voice is like the sweetest song and he's smile so very, very special. Beyond that there are no words to describe Jesus.

We human beings are so busy providing for this earthly life that all is forgotten that there is an afterlife.

1 John 2: 3-4: "And hereby we do know that we know him, if we keep his commandments."

If we say we know him and do not keep his commandments we are liars and the truth is not in us.

Romans 14: 10: ". . . for we shall all stand before the judgment seat of Christ."

Hebrews 9: 27: "And as it is appointed unto men once to die, but after this the judgment."

Truly the love of God is perfect in us, if we keep his word. If we say we abide in him we ought to walk as he walked.

The *backbiting* and *unforgiving* of other Christians is one of the biggest reasons why people who accept Jesus Christ as Savior, and go to church still end up in hell.

Humbleness, total surrender and trust are the keys to heaven. Grab hold of these keys and reject the desires of the world. In this world we live but through baptism (crucified in the flesh) and we are no longer part of the world. Many Christians are not ready to humble themselves all because of pride and would rather stay in darkness. This means they are far, far away from God and cannot find their way to heaven.

Please do not harden your heart to the love of God.

Mark 8:17: ". . . Is your heart still hardened?"

Hebrews 3: 13: ". . . lest any of you be hardened through the deceitfulness of sin."

We are being shown that Jesus does not just love, but is love. Through us, his children, he is sending out warnings.

Amos 4: 12: ". . . prepare to meet thy God . . ."

Luke 1: 76: ". . . for thou shalt go before the face of the Lord to prepare his ways."

PREPARE!!!!

The End is near and God will pour his wrath out upon the earth. Don't grieve the Holy Spirit; come unto Jesus because tomorrow may be too late.

If you are serious about becoming a child of God, then follow these six steps to salvation.

1) *Acknowledge*—realize and admit you have acted wrongly against God's laws. Read the Ten Commandments in Exodus 20: 3-17. Are you a good person? Romans 3: 23 "For all have sinned and come short of the glory of God." Luke 18: 13: ". . . God be merciful to me a sinner."

2) *Repent*—feel honest regret for these wrong-doings. Luke 13: 3: ". . . I tell you. Unless you change your hearts and lives you will be destroyed . . ."

3) *Confess*—admit your mistakes. 1 John 1: 9: "If we confess our sins, he is faithful and just to forgive us our sins and to cleanse us from all unrighteousness." Romans 10: 9: ". . . if thou shalt confess with thy mouth the Lord Jesus, and shalt believe in thine heart that God hath raised him from the dead, thou shalt be saved."

4) *Forsake*—try your best not to do them again. Isaiah 55: 7: "The wicked should stop doing wrong and they should return to the Lord so he may have mercy on them. They should come to our God, because he will freely forgive

them" The Lord tells us in Hebrews 13: 5: ". . . I will never leave thee nor forsake thee."

5) *Believe*—know Jesus died for you. John 3: 16: "For God so loved the world, that he gave his only begotten Son, that whosoever believeth in him should not perish but have everlasting life." Mark 16: 16: "He that believeth and is baptized shall be saved . . ."

6) *Receive*—ask Jesus to be part of your life. Acts 10: 43: ". . . through his name whosoever believeth in him shall receive remission of sins."

Say this prayer—Lord Jesus. I am a sinner and I need your forgiveness. The doorway to my heart is open to you and I receive you as my Lord and Savior. I believe in my heart and confess with my lips, that Jesus Christ is my Lord and Savior. Come into my heart, Lord Jesus; take my life for I now surrender it all to you. Thank you for forgiving my sins and showing me I am special to you. Please take control of my life and use me in whatever you want me to do, for my life is in your hands from this day forward. Lord, from this moment forward, I will live according to your word, the Bible, and will serve you with all my heart. Thank you, Lord, for taking away my sins and giving me everlasting life.

In the name of Jesus, I pray.

Amen.

2 Corinthians 5: 17 tells us; ". . . if any man be in Christ, he is a new creature, old things have passed away; behold all things are become new."

Now that you have received or rededicated your life to God you should:

1) Read your Bible everyday to get to know Jesus better. 2 Timothy 2: 15: "Make every effort to give yourself to God as the kind of person he will accept. Be a worker who is not ashamed and who uses the true teaching in the right way." Psalms 119: 105: "Thy word is a lamp unto my feet and a light unto my path."

2) *Talk to Jesus,* sometimes in prayer and other times as if you were talking to a best friend. You can talk to Jesus anytime or anywhere. 1 Thessalonians 5: 17: "Pray without ceasing." Colossians 4: 2: "Continue in prayer . . ." 1 Peter 5: 7: "Casting all your cares upon him, for he careth for you." Praying everyday keeps your faith built up and helps you resist the devil." James 4: 7: "Submit yourselves to God. Resist the devil and he will flee from you."

3) *Be baptized,* worship, fellowship and serve other Christians in a church where Christ is preached and the Bible is the final authority. Matthew 28: 19: "So go and make followers of all people in the world. Baptize them in the name of the Father and the son and the Holy Ghost."

Hebrews 10: 25: "You should not stay away from church meetings, as some are doing, but you should meet together and encourage each other." 2 Timothy 3: 16: "All scripture is given by God and is useful for teaching, for showing people what is wrong in their lives, for correcting faults and for teaching how to live right."

4) *Tell others about Christ.*

Mark 16: 15: "Go ye into all the world and preach the gospel to every creature." 1 Corinthians 9: 16: "Telling the Good News does not give me any reason for bragging. Telling the Good News is my duty— something I must do. And how terrible it will be for me if I do not tell the Good News." Romans 1: 16: "For I am not ashamed of the gospel of Christ; for it is a terrible evil to turn away from the Lord your God."

5) *Obey the Ten Commandments.* Exodus 20: 3-17.

   a) Thou shalt not have any other gods before me.
   b) Thou shalt not make unto thee any graven images . . ."
   c) Thou shalt not take the name of the Lord thy God in vain . . ."
   d) Remember the Sabbath day, to keep it holy . . ."
   e) Honor thy father and mother that thy days may be long upon the land . . ."

f) Thou shalt not kill.

g) Thou shalt not commit adultery.

h) Thou shalt not steal.

i) Thou shalt not bear false witness against thy neighbor."

j) Thou shalt not covet thy neighbor's house, thou shalt not covet they neighbors wife, nor his manservant, nor his maidservant, nor his ox, nor his ass, nor anything that is thy neighbor's."

These commandments were written by the Lord for all to obey.

In Matthew 22: 37-40, God gives us two special commandments. One is to love the Lord with all thy heart and all thy soul and with all thy mind. The second is to love thy neighbor as thyself.

In this world, of ours, we get discouraged and sometime we wonder if the Lord answers.

When prayers don't seem to be answered than God has a reason and we need to accept his answer. Because he knows what is best for us and will help us through everything we go through. Here are some examples.

1) Lord, take away this pain. He tells us 'no' that it is not for me to take away, but it's up to us to give it up. Jeremiah 15: 18: "Why is my pain perpetual . . ."

2) Lord, make my handicapped child whole. Sometimes he will answer and tell us that her body is only temporary, but her spirit is whole.

3) Lord, give me patience. No! He says. Patience is a by-product of tribulations; it is earned, not granted. James 1: 4: "But let patience have its perfect work, that you may be perfect and complete . . ."

4) Lord, give me happiness. No! I give you blessings. Happiness is up to you. Proverbs 16: 20: ". . . And whoever trusts in the Lord, happy is he."

5) Lord, spare me pain. No! Suffering brings you closer to me and draws you apart from worldly cares. Psalms 55: 4: "My heart is sore pained within me . . ."

6) Lord, make my spirit grow. No! On your own you must grow but for you to be fruitful I will prune you. 1 John 4: 13: "Hereby know we that dwell in him, and he in us, because he hath given us of the Spirit."

7) Lord, give me all the things to enjoy life. No! I will give you life so all these things you may enjoy. 1 Timothy 6:17: "trust . . . in the living God, who giveth us richly all things to enjoy."

8) Lord, help me to love others as much as you love me. *AHH!!!* You finally have the right idea. John 15: 12: ". . . That ye love one another, as I have loved you."

CHAPTER 9

D O YOU KNOW WHAT you will experience when you are dying?

What will you see immediately after your death?

After that, where will your soul be?

If someone were to ask you, 'Where do you think you will go after death? Would you be sure of the answer? Would your soul go to heaven or hell?' When I was asked that question I was not sure how to answer it. But now beyond a shadow of a doubt I do. I am a child of God and as he's child my home will be heaven.

Heaven seemed like a fairy tale and I found it hard to understand and accept. I was unsure what it meant to accept Jesus Christ as my Savior.

It was during a revival that I accepted Jesus Christ with all my heart.

After I got home from the revival I felt an urge to fast, which I did. During my fasting I experienced the power of the Holy Spirit and my body warmed up.

Acts 1: 8: "But ye shall receive power, after that the Holy Ghost is come upon you . . ."

John 1: 12: "But as many as received him, to them gave he power to become sons (and daughters) of God."

Micah 3: 8: "But truly I am full of power by the spirit of the Lord . . ."

Once the power of the Holy Spirit came upon me I felt unspeakable peace, joy and rest in my heart. I was a new creation and I knew beyond a shadow of a doubt that I had eternal life. Through fasting and prayer I felt I had received the assurance of Jesus and had full confidence I would go to heaven when I died.

What message does God have for the church today?

How do we recognize the schemes of the enemy?

How do we live in victory Jesus purchased for us on the cross?

Have you had a child that dies? Where and what are they doing right now? What is taking place? Does the spirit and soul of an infant exist?

CHAPTER 10

*E*VERY OUNCE OF OXYGEN left my body and I suddenly descended into a horrible pit. How could this be happening? *I am a child of God.* As I descended all I could hear was screaming and moaning. Jesus was waiting for me in this horrible pit. He was there because he had chosen me to see and hear what happens to people who die without him. *Lost forever!!!*

Jesus said to me, 'My precious child, I want you to witness the devastation, the torture, torments these lost souls will suffer, so you may go back and warn them.

There is another side of hell that people need to know about. *Outer Darkness!!* This outer darkness is located in the second heaven which is an exit for all who put their trust in God. This exit is called the third heaven.

The second heaven is in this outer darkness is where hell is. In this present day and hour only a handful of people alive have seen this side of hell. Many, many preachers that serve me, there on earth are committing sins in their lives. They don't think

I know about their sins, but I know everything. This outer darkness awaits all who are hypocritical and unrepentant. I want you to tell people about the real existence and the outer darkness of hell and its horrible punishments.'

This chamber is shrouded in total darkness and the smells are horrendous. In this total darkness people were chained and tortured in horrible ways. The pain and horror of hell coursed through my body.

If being in this chamber, of total darkness, wasn't enough I was led by a strange, foul creature that emitted the illusion of a person. As I stood rooted in the spot where I was and he demanded that I follow him. We walked for awhile until we came to a wall with a door. Entering through this door I could see a giant room filled with cubicles, from the ground up and as far as the eye could see. Every cubicle represented someone who was recompensing for their deeds. Individual people were in various stages of anguish, boredom and other hideous torments. These were spirits who were afraid of the light that stayed in shadows. Because of their actions they had done in human existence they felt unworthy to look into the light. These spirits were chained to the consequences of their acts.

I looked around and found numerous creatures were laughing at me. These hideous creatures grabbed hold of me and took turns raping me. I screamed out to God, but all I heard were these demons laughing at me.

Into the abysmal depths my soul fell, so very, very deep. I was pressed between two burning planks, sharp nails and red hot irons piercing into my flesh. Creatures of every shape and size were trying to pull my tongue out, but couldn't. The torture I was suffering caused such agony I felt my eyes pop from their sockets and a sickening stench permeated and corrupted everything.

Discarnate hordes of ghostly beings roamed back and forth. These ugly indescribable demons taunted me with these words, 'We've got you, and we've got you.' These demons were the most frustrated, angriest and most miserable beings I had ever laid eyes on. Throwing people off a high cliff and into the lake of fire was hilarious to them, watching them writher in agony but never dying. Arms were upheld with flesh dripping off and their clothes were consumed and unmistakable traces of fire clung to their bodies.

Revelation 14: 10-11: "The same drink of the wine of the wrath of God, which is poured out without mixture into the cup of his indignation; and he shall be tormented with fire and brimstone in the presence of the holy angels and in the presence of the Lamb. And smoke of their torture ascendeth up forever and ever: and they have no rest day nor night . . ."

The Bible presents Satan as a powerful being who is the active enemy of God. Hebrew word Satan means "adversary," as does the Greek satanas.

God pleaded with me to warn others about hell.

The almighty Jesus took my human spirit and soul out of my body and there I stood before him, susceptible.

Through Gods Holy Spirit I was allowed to see almost two hundred rooms in hell, the pits of hell, flames and fires of hell and the lake of fire. God showed me individuals tormented in hell by flames of the unquenchable fire. He also showed me demons and familiar spirits. Lucifer, the fallen angel, also known as Satan and the devil was shown to me. Revelation 12: 9: "And the great dragon was cast out, that old serpent, called the Devil and Satan, which deceiveth the whole world: he was cast out into the earth and his angels were cast out with him." Some scholars refer to Lucifer as Beelzebub 9prince of demons). But in the Christian world he is known as Lucifer, the fallen cherubim.

Within my heart, mind and soul depression became deeper and deeper and it burnt so hot it consumed me.

Satan and his evil demons had taken over every realm of my life. Ever present was the voice of Satan telling me I was not worthy to living and that I should commit suicide because no one cared and I would be better off dead. Ever prevalent in my mind was the thought of suicide. My survival trance intensified to a frightening pitch at the brink of my attempt. I felt extended beyond my capacity for survival. My emotions of anger and grief had overwhelmed me. My ability to consider my options had been cut short and I seen my future through a narrow tunnel, at the end there was only one possible outcome. Suicide was the only channel in which I could find relief from my overwhelming rage.

My soul separated from my body and I was transported to Heaven's gate, but I was barred from entering. Before me was a large screen which showed my life in a three dimensional slide show.

A figure, which looked like a man, came towards me and told me he had been instructed to show me another sphere.

In the twinkling of an eye I was standing near a shoreline in front of a lake of fire. The Bible tells us about the lake of fire in Revelation 21: 8: ". . . the lake which burns with fire and brimstone."

Next to me stood an ominous figure, the devil and he motioned for me to follow him. Pouring through my veins I felt an inner turmoil which made me feel like I was suffocating. Fear enveloped my soul. From behind the devil came screaming like no other: screams from the soul. I couldn't pull back for it seemed like a huge magnet was steadily pulling me into the lake of fire. I screamed and screamed but to no avail. Satan wore red and black, but his face looked like a living skeleton. Negative feelings emitted from him. Large wings sprouted from his sides and his eyes were a glowing, piercing red. The wings on Satan's sides were so enormous that when he opened them, they filled the whole room. I couldn't move because I was so terrified. With his face next to mine he said he said he had been waiting for me and that I must go with him. The devil took me into a different realm.

Where am I? Where am I?

Into a place of total darkness Satan had led me to. Here I was immersed in darkness and in every direction it seemed to continue and seemed like it would never end. It was not just blackness and an endless void, but an absence of light. This total darkness enveloped me.

Looking around I suddenly came face to face with a creature with no expression showing on his face. There was no warmth or intelligence in his eyes for his eyes were cold and steely.

"You must be suicide," the creature said.

By an unseen and undefined power I was sucked deeper and deeper into utter darkness. I landed on the edge of a shadowy realm, suspended in the darkness that extended to the limits of my sight.

Purgatory!!! (any condition or place of temporary suffering or punishment). I knew this was where I was.

In this realm there were people of all ages and nationalities crouching and roaming about and I could hear them mumbling. From deep within the utter darkness radiated in a way I could feel. Everyone was self-absorbed, caught up in their own misery. There was no mental or emotional exchange because they were caught up in themselves. They could communicate with one another but were incapacitated by the darkness. I became aware of voices, even though thoughts were the mode of communication in this realm. Reaching out with my mind for information, a tremendous disappointment filled me. By posing a question I could feel and know about everything around me. The possibilities were endless of learning, but there was no way to use the knowledge I had gained. Looking at the pathetic souls I realized I no longer felt the way they did.

I want to live!!!I want to live!!!

Once I came to the realization that I wanted to live the powerful source that had transported me to this dark prison now returned to liberate me.

Suddenly I felt the presence of another, the same presence that had been with me when I first crossed over into death and reviewed my life. He had been there all along but only now was I able to perceive him. I could sense his powerful, gentle personality. Through the darkness came bits of light, with the power of an all-consuming love and the ray of light penetrated me with and incredible force. This ray of light had an entirely new dimension of pure compassion, complete and perfect empathy. The presence by my side understood and felt my pain, as if he had walked in my shoes. He understood how to guide me through.

The darkness dispelled and I found myself in the most magnificent place I had ever seen.

I now stood on the streets of gold and a light drew me closer and closer.

Revelation 21: 21: ". . . and the streets of the city was pure gold . . ."

The center of the universe seemed to radiate from this light. I could not feel my feet touching the ground—it seemed like one minute I was in one spot and within the next minute I was transported to the light. Many angels and I flew together.

What a spectacular and sight. Never could I imagine a place so beautiful and so peaceful. Every flower imaginable grew in beautiful gardens. Little water falls flowed with a kaleidoscope of color. This sight left me breathless. Standing there on the streets of gold I was surrounded with love and compassion. So many loved ones and friends stood there welcoming me and making me feel accepted, loved and wanted. A light that was bright, beautiful and pure broke off and a ray from the source came towards me. As the light reached my body waves of love permeated me making me feel very safe and giving me comfort and warmth to my soul. This physical light gave off living emotions. Pure peace came with another wave and yet another gave me pure joy.

'Where am I?'

'Am I out of my body?'

'Is this real?'

'Am I standing in the here or am I having a bizarre dream?'

'Am I in the presence of the Lord?'

The answer to this last question was *yes*, I was in the presence of the Lord.

Moving in the presence of the Lord a door opened to a new world—green pastures, like none I had ever seen, crystal clear streams, rolling majestic hills and pure blue skies above. Off in the distance mountains in all their majesty, fields interspersed with the most beautiful flowers you could lay eyes on and trees in all their glory. This is perfect creation.

1 John 1: 5: ". . . God is light and in him there is no darkness at all."

There was no evil, no darkness nor any sorrow, for this was pure light. As I stood in the presence of God, he spoke my name. He knew, he knew my name.

Standing there I became aware of the presence/existence of God and my accountability. A great blessing was that we could communicate on a spiritual level. My thoughts were known to him even before I spoke. God knew everything I had done in my life, the lies, deceiving others, the sexual encounters I had and much more but yet he stilled loves me.

NO!!NO!! I didn't want God seeing the ugliness in my life. Standing in front of this pure light I felt totally exposed and I desired to move back to the darkness where I belonged. My thought was that I had been brought to heaven by mistake. I started backing away but suddenly a wave of light swept through me and pure unadultered love permeated me.

How could God love me?

During my life I had sexual encounters, had cursed, taken the Lord's name in vain, disobeyed and much more. There was no way I had been a good person—but no matter what I said these waves of unconditional love permeated me. Surrounded by this pure love I cried uncontrollably. As I stood in God's presence a radiance of love flowed from him to me. I was really surprised that God had totally forgiven me and accepted me as I was.

Ephesians 3: 19: ". . . the love of Christ, which passeth knowledge, that ye might be filled with all the fullness of God."

In a gentle and loving voice God explained to me that suicide was the worst thing I could do that he had given the commandment that 'thou shalt not kill' and that meant even the taking of my own life.

Anger and frustration filled my heart because I had thrown in the towel and cut myself off from him and his guidance.

"Lord, my life is hard."

"If you think life is hard—it is nothing compared to what awaits you if you commit suicide. I have ordained your life and you cannot skip parts of your life."

"Why is there so much pain on earth?" I ask the Lord.

His reply to me was; "Don't you know I have the power to take away pain?"

With the power of an all consuming love, God's ray of light penetrated me with incredible force. Such a pure love. He understood my life and pain. God knew everything about how to guide me through life and he showed me how my different choices could either produce bitterness or new growth.

God grieved and ached for my sorrow and pain. His greatest desire was to help me.

As I was flooded with his love and actual pain he bore for me, my spiritual eyes were opened. God knew where I stood in the need of mercy.

I knew heaven is where I belonged—that God created me to live here and I knew I was home and I basked in the enormous joy.

But as I was about to step over the threshold and into the city of gold, God stepped in front of me.

'Lord, please, I want to stay for I have no one or nothing to go back to.'

The Lord stood in front of me, barring the doorway. He told me, 'You must see things in a different light. Begin to see through the eyes of peace, joy, and forgiveness, from my heavenly perspective, not earthly perspective. If you stay here there will be people who will not get a chance to hear about me.

My plans I have set forth for you have not yet been performed by you.'

God went on to tell me I must warn all the Christians who will not make the rapture.

The trumpets blew proclaiming the coming of the Lord coming to take his bride home.

1 Corinthians 15: 52: "in a moment, in the twinkling of an eye . . . For the trumpet shall sound . . ."

It shocked me to see so many Christians failing the rapture. I could not recognize anyone—which was good.

Darkness reigned even though it was daytime. It's a strange sensation hearing strange voices from everywhere.

The Holy Spirit, I realized, was no longer on the earth thus causing the darkness.

Demons were seen everywhere and people were screaming in fear.

Due to the lack of knowledge, because of indecency, unseemliness, witchcraft, jealousy, outburst of anger, selfish ambitions, disagreements, adultery, fornication, the worshiping of idols, hatred, quarreling, envy, heresies, murder, drunkenness, competition, rejecting of our fellow believers and the lack of love many will miss their goal.

Galatians 5: 16-25: ". . . Live by following the Spirit. Then you will not do what your sinful selves want. Our sinful selves want what is against the Spirit and the Spirit wants what is against our sinful selves. The two are against each other, so you cannot do just as you please. But if the Spirit is leading you, you are not under the law. The wrong things the sinful self does are clear: being sexually unfaithful, not being pure, taking part in sexual sins, worshipping gods, doing witchcraft, hating, making trouble, being jealous, being angry, being selfish, making people angry with each other, causing divisions among people, feeling envy, being drunk, having wild and wasteful parties and doing other things like these. I warn you now as I warned you before: Those who do these things will not inherit God's kingdom. But the Spirit produces the fruit of love, joy, peace, patience, kindness, goodness, faithfulness, gentleness, self-control. There is no law that says these things are wrong. Those who belong to Christ Jesus have crucified their sinful selves. They have given up their old selfish feelings and the evil things they wanted to do. We get our new life from the spirit, so we should follow the Spirit."

1 Peter 1: 18-19: "You know that in the past you were living in a worthless way . . . But you were saved from that useless life. You were bought, not with something that ruins . . . but with the precious blood of Christ . . ."

With an inner certainty I know God is real and he loves me. John 3: 16: "For God so loved the world, that he gave his only begotten Son, that whosoever believeth in him should not perish but have everlasting life."

With a heart full of sadness, I was sent back to earth.

I was bound by what I thought when I died. In morality the more solid my thoughts became the more I acted upon them allowing the darkness to surround me. The more solid my thoughts became the more damning they were.

Romans 8: 6-7: "If people's thinking is controlled by the sinful self, there is death. If people's thinking is controlled by the sinful self, they are against God . . ."

I found that our mind and conscience is defiled when we let Satan have control of our lives.

Long before I died I had been in hell, although I never realized it because I had escaped many of the consequences—that is up to the point I died.

Just before awakening I saw an angel. He seemed like a giant of a man, but he was so beautiful. My desire was to get closer to him but as I got to the feet of this angel, the sky opened and heavenly light poured down upon my body and my heart melted with pure love for Jesus. He was and still is my greatest friend and I had forgotten him.

Many things happened as life went on, for God works in mysterious ways.

The Bible tells us in 1 John 4: 8: ". . . God is love."

No human beings will ever understand fully the greatness of God's love until we live with him in eternity.

Believers trust me!!!

Hell is real and if we don't let go of all our sins, many of which were listed above and allow God to cleanse us and if we don't obey his word—*Hell will be your destination.*

The New Testament gives us numerous scriptures on the subject of hell.

Matthew 5: 22: ". . . but whosoever shall say Thou fool shall be in danger of hell fire.

Matthew 11: 23: "And thou, Capernaum, which art exalted unto heaven, shalt be brought down to hell . . ."

Matthew 13: 42: "And shall cast them into a furnace of fire . . ."

Matthew 23: 33: ". . . how can ye escape the damnation of hell?"

Revelation 19: 20: ". . . These both were cast alive into a lake of fire burning with brimstone."

These are but a few of the scriptures that refer to hell.

CHAPTER 11

URING MY DAILY BIBLE study I read in Psalms 91: 11-12 that the angels will carry you upon their hands and no evil will befall you.

This scripture came to mind later that afternoon when heart trouble that I had been bothered with for some time flared up. The pain I experienced was excruciating.

My husband called an ambulance and I was rushed to the hospital. There they administered a drug I was allergic to even after being told of the allergy.

It wasn't long before I went into anaphylactic shock. My throat closed up, my heart stopped beating and I flat-lined (died).suddenly I could see everything that was going on in the emergency room. *Code blue—Code blue* the doctors were screaming. I seen doctors and nurses feverously working on me trying to get a heart beat but to them it was a losing battle.

Before the last breath took me, I ask the Lord to take me into his care. After I said that all pain and anxiety left me and I left my bed in perfect health and was surrounded by a majestic light full of excellence and comfort. There were hundreds of people standing in line and I could make out the sex gender but there were no recognizable features.

God is light but suddenly I felt his wrath. I now realized that I was standing before God in judgment. I was in one of the lines and the lines were moving but I was not walking. The line stopped and I was before the throne of God. Kneeling before him I could feel his fury and knew I was damned. As I lifted my head and looked over I saw my siblings and it shamed me that I had done very unpleasant things to them. My humiliation was beyond relief. The pain was so great I begged for it to stop. The pain stopped, for a second, but started again with more intensity. I was no longer feeling my humiliation and pain but that of my siblings. This was a taste of hell. I begged and begged for the intensity from their pain to stop but it wouldn't. Their pain was so profound I would have given anything for it to stop.

The line begins moving again but I knew I wasn't going to heaven. I had been given a preview of what was in store for me and that was hell. I cried as terror filled my heart that *I was going to hell.* Once again the line stopped. A small, still voice told me I was going back. A relief flooded my heart as I realized that I wasn't going to hell. I understood I would be carrying the pain of my siblings until the day I took my final breath. But carrying this pain will be a constant reminder of what I say to people can really hurt them.

While in heaven, I now found myself being lifted from the line, by three heavenly beings in long, white flowing robes. They cupped me in their hands and carried me. As they gently carried me away, I looked into their faces but I could not recognize them.

I must have died.

I ask these beings where they were taking me and with unspoken words they relayed to me that I was being taken to the City of the Great King. These heavenly beings treated me with great respect like I was the daughter of the King or a princess.

I knew I was in heaven. In comparison to heaven, everything I had seen on earth was dull. The music was harmonious and nothing like it on earth. While in heaven my spirit was filled with joy, love, and with ultimate purity of the Holy Spirit that was filling me. It was while I was in heaven that I learned a deeper meaning of God's love. Throughout my heavenly experience I had a distinct feeling that someone was close by because I experienced an intense feeling of love.

There was no tunnel nor did I see any family members but went directly to the City of Lights and was presented to the Great King. The king treated me like a prodigal daughter coming home. In Luke 15: 11-32 it tells of a son who took his portion of inheritance and left and went to a far away country. He devoured all his money and was left feeding and eating with the swine. Finally he came to his senses and returned home. Once home his father greeted him with open arms. This was the same greeting I got from the King and I was no longer a prodigal daughter but safe in the arms of God. His emotions were intense and he let me know he was in love with me and everyone who professed his name. He said I could stay if I chose to but I ask to return to my body because there was so much to do for his namesake. Before he returned me to my earthly body he showed me off and honored me. This was confusing because I should be honoring him.

Within a short time I was back in my body.

If only others could see the glorious city awaiting them and the great place he has been building for the ones who have place their trust in Jesus. Christ Jesus is very eager to show us what awaits us and to show off to his heavenly Father.

God is in love with his people and we are considered courageous by angels who surround us at the command of the King.

Don't despair!! Lift up your head for your deliverance is nearer than you think.

John 14: 21: "He that hath my commandments and keepeth them, he it is that loveth me and he that loveth me shall be loved by my Father and I will love him and manifest myself to him."

Matthew 24: 33: "So likewise ye, when ye shall see all things, know that it is near, even at the doors."

Matthew 25: 13: "Watch therefore, for ye know neither the day nor the hour wherein the Son of man cometh."

There is one thing I want all to know—I am a converted sinner who is serving God to the best of my ability with a pure and whole heart.

Not many people want to go to hell but everyone wants to go to heaven. People think they can go to heaven with little or no prepared work

NOT SO!!!

CHAPTER 12

I WAS EXTREMELY EXHAUSTED AND felt I could no longer stay awake, so I laid down for a nap. This was to be no ordinary nap.

NO!! This would be something I would never forget. My body was lifted up and transported to a different sphere. I slid into something that resembled an underground coal mine. Dark, oh, so dark and cold.

Lamentations 3: 53-57: My enemies "Tried to kill me in the pit, they threw stones at me. Water came up over my head and I said "I am going to die." I called out to the Lord from the bottom of the pit. You heard me calling. "Do not close your ears and ignore my gasps and shouts." You came near when I called to you, you said, "Don't be afraid." From the bottom of the pit I saw a flicker of light. My entire spirit and body was housed there.

I said to myself; "You're dead."

There were no signs indicating where I was but in my spirit, I knew.

While in the pit I knew I was in the company of very ugly, evil, demonic, deformed, scary-looking unexplainable creatures. Evil surrounded me on all sides. Dark clouds approached me from every side. Demons came from every direction and stared at my body. I had died and went to hell and now I had no chance of escaping. I cried out to God for help but received no answer.

"Oh!! Lord, what have I done to deserve being sent to hell?"

In a split second I heard a voice and it told me that in my life I had been stingy, self-centered, mean, rude to others and very, very selfish.

Suddenly I saw what looked like a wide screen television in front of me. I saw these words, "*This Is Your Life!!*" The movie showed me the things I had done on earth. There were more times than I count that I had lied to my parents and others, a time when I had stolen a compact from a five and dime store. It was broke and I didn't think they would mind. Other scenes showed the times I had been cruel to my siblings, times I had lied to get what I wanted, the sexual encounters that were unpleasing to God, backbiting and so many more. As I watched these scenes, I wept bitterly before God.

"Lord, forgive me," I wept. "Remove me from this pit."

With a burst of energy I was sucked up and brought back to my body.

For many weeks I did not tell anyone of this experience. It weighed heavily on my soul, so I decided to tell my psychologist, who was also a minister of a church. I thought he would understand about this kind of experience. But telling him was a bad mistake. After I explained this experience to him he looked at me like I had lost my mind and then said to me that I was a paranoid schizophrenic. He told me that no one believed in those things. His statement cut to the depths of my soul because I knew what I had experienced.

This experience happened shortly after I was saved so I had no idea why God had chosen to send me to hell. Curiosity got the best of me so I ask the Lord; "Lord, why me? Why wait so long before sending me to hell?"

God's answer came swiftly as he said to me; "I did not send you to hell because you were a sinner but I sent you on behalf of sinners, so you could be a witness. I allowed you to experience this so you would know for yourself that there is a hell and that it really does exist. I want you to tell others to repent from their sins and I want you to share your experiences in hell. They must be told hell is a place of tortures, torments and extreme cruelty. Plead with them to give their lives to me before it is too late. Go out now and witness and warn people of the horrors of hell."

Romans 6: 10: ". . . He died to sin once for all . . ."

Ezekiel 18: 4: ". . . The soul who sins shall die."

Sinners repent for time is drawing near. 1 John 1: 9: tells us "If we confess our sins, He is faithful and just to forgive us our sins and to cleanse us from all unrighteousness." Please, give your hearts to God so you will be prepared to stand before the throne of God as a sinner saved by grace. Hell is no place you want to be.

What is a witness? The dictionary tells us it is a person able to give evidence, or a person who saw something happen.

I had seen and experienced the horrors of hell.

From within the darkness I heard lost souls crying and begging; "Save us please—this place is unbearable and we are in great pain and suffering." My heart became overwhelmed with sorrow. A voice penetrated the darkness and said; "This is hell." I had read about the existence of hell, in my daily Bible study, but never did I think I would see it with my own eyes that it was real.

Isaiah 14: 9: "Hell from beneath is excited about you. To meet you at your coming; It stirs up the dead for you . . ."

There are four words that describe hell.

The first one is a Hebrew word, *"Sheol"* which is a world of the dead or grave. This place was where the souls of the ungodly and godly men and women came when they died centuries ago.

Isaiah 5: 14: "Therefore hell hath enlarged herself and opened her mouth without measure . . ."

Job 17: 16: "Will they go down to the gates of Sheol . . . ?"

Psalms 16:10: "For you will not leave my soul in Sheol . . ."

The second word is a Greek word and that word is *"Hades."* Hades the unseen world. Hades is the place of departed souls and spirits or where a sinner goes after death.

Acts 2: 27: "For you will not leave my soul in Hades . . ."

Matthew 16: 18: ". . . and the gates of Hades will not prevail against it."

God spoke and said; "Before I was crucified and rose again Hades was divided into two sections, which were than separated by a large impassable gulf, which I created." The upper side of Hades was called Abrahams Bosom and Paradise.

In Matthew 16: 22-26 we are told of a rich man and Lazarus. The rich man died and awoke in Hades and was tormented.

The room of the cursed is the portion of what was Abrahams Bosom in Hades. In the cursed Paradise of the Outer Darkness of Hell, it was very pleasant. Running through it were streams of water with green trees. It reminded me of a well-maintained park. This place contained the souls of all the people who had died and put their faith and trust in God during the Old Testament period, up until the crucifixion and resurrection. The human spirits here, in Paradise of

Hades, were conscious. These spirits were not soul-sleeping, they were quite alive. During the three days between the crucifixion Christ spent in Hell preaching to them.

The old prophets rejoiced because of God's presence in Hades for the three days. God removed these prophets and other believers and took them to a New Paradise, which is the third heaven. The New Paradise is also called Abraham's Bosom. For the ones who would not put their trust in God when they died, their human souls went to Hades, where many torments and agonizing fires exist. In this part of Hell is placed the 'Fiery Pits of Hades.'

The third word describing Hell is *Tartaros,* signifying the infernal region. This is a place of severe punishment and judgments for all who disobey the Holy Word. Tartaros has many jail cells. Only once in the Bible was this mentioned.

2 Peter 2: 4: "For if God spared not the angels that sinned, but cast them down to hell and delivered them into chains of darkness to be reserved unto judgment."

The Everyday Bible states it this way; "When angels sinned, God did not let them go free without punishment. He sent them to hell and put them in caves of darkness where they were being held for judgment."

This portion of hell held the angels who sexually sinned with the women, on earth, before Noah's flood.

Jude 1:6: "And the angels which kept not their first estate, but left their own habitation, he hath reserved in everlasting chains under darkness into the judgment of the great day." These are fallen angels who left their first estate that are bound in chains, awaiting the Great White Throne of judgment day.

Zophos is Greek for darkness, blackness and gloomy surrounding mist.

Choshek is a Hebrew word for darkness. Also it means misery, destruction, death, sorrow and wickedness.

Matthew 8: 12: "But the children of the kingdom shall be cast out into Outer Darkness, there shall be weeping and gnashing of teeth."

Fourth word for hell is a Greek language word *Gehenna,* signifying the place of torment.

If any person on earth completely rejects the Lord Jesus Christ when they die they will be brought down to Hades and burned in Gehenna where the fire is never quenched.

Matthew 5: 22: ". . . if you are angry with a brother or sister, you will be judged. If you say bad things to a brother or sister, you will be judged by council. And if you call someone a fool you will be in danger of the fire of hell."

Matthew 5: 29: ". . . It is better to lose one part of the body than to have your whole body thrown into hell."

Gehenna burns twenty-four hours a day and was used as a public—garbage dumping site for the people of Jerusalem. Here dead animals were set on fire, filling the air with a horrible unbearable stench which polluted the air. This site was located in the valley of Hinnow, on the outside walls of Jerusalem. It is a valley W. and S.W. of Jerusalem.

Gehenna is spoken of several times in the Bible.

Revelation 2: 11: ". . . He that overcometh shall not be hurt of the second death."

Revelation 19: 20: ". . . These both were cast alive into a lake of fire burning with brimstone."

Revelation 20: 14: "And death and hell were cast into the lake of fire. This is the second death."

These three are but a handful of verses talking about hell.

The Lake of fire was given the name Gehenna because of the twenty-four hour burning. This place will burn and torment human souls and spirits of the sinners who willfully reject God. Gehenna is prepared for the Devil, his angels and for any human beings that has no desire to love and obey Jesus as their only God.

Matthew 25: 41: "Then shall he say also unto them on the left hand, Depart from me, ye cursed into everlasting fire, prepared for the devil and his angels."

Matthew 28: 20: ". . . I am with you always even unto the end of the world."

John 14: 27: "Peace I leave with you, my peace I give unto you: not as the world giveth, give I unto you. Let not your heart be troubled, neither let it be afraid."

Matthew 16: 24: "If any man will come after me, let him deny himself and take up the cross and follow me."

Every person who puts their trust in God will be able to recognize His divine, holy presence and will be able to hear his voice any way he chooses to speak them.

John 10: 4: "And when he putteth forth his own sheep, he goeth before them and the sheep follow him, for they know his voice."

I ask God why these people were suffering in such a horrible place.

It was as if the Lord knew my thought because he answered and said: "while on earth these people did not accept me as their Lord. Upon their death they were brought here."

Looking towards heaven I shouted: "Angels, immediately protect my body, please." I never knew what angels looked like, but the instant I shouted they appeared, immediately coming down to protect my body.

Ahead of me was a giant, black pit with unquenchable flames of fire. This pit was solid rock and it was frightening and horrifying. Speaking to me a voice said: "This is the bottomless pit where the devil will be bound one day.

Revelation 20: 2-3: "The angel grabbed the dragon, that old snake who is the devil and Satan and tied him up for a thousand years. Then he threw him into a bottomless pit and closed it . . ."

From a high height I saw people coming and going, sleeping, working, eating and spending but they were not content with their lives. This discontentment led to frustration, misery and suffering. As I saw this, my heart saddened with grief for the world's suffering and tears rolled down my cheeks.

CHAPTER 13

*A*S MY SPIRIT LEFT my body I found myself at the end of a golden staircase with golden railings on each side. From heaven came a strong beam of light and from this light an angel appeared and I was taken up to heaven. All these saints welcomed me warmly to heaven which emotionally touched me. No one rejected or paid attention to me because I was just an ordinary housewife on earth.

2 Corinthians 15: 5: ". . . be ye steadfast, unmovable, always abounding in the work of the Lord, forasmuch as ye know that your labour is not in vain in the Lord."

From heaven to earth I saw angels flying up and down and as they did they passed the Lord. Winged angels wearing white robes with golden belts lined the staircase from top to bottom. The angels had white shining hair, faces shining like the morning star and their eyes were like two powerful lanterns. These angels were singing Hallelujah!! Amen!! Praise the Lord!!!

The color of shiny copper chips was their arms and legs.

Another set of angels, these without wings surrounded the winged angels. Together they sang in heavenly language which after a moment I understood was the words of a psalm. "O Worthy are you Lord of all glory and praise."

At the top of the staircase I saw a very brilliant light. It was like an incredible light that could only belong to a heavenly body and this light would be harmful to your eyes on earth. This light was extremely bright, warm, calming, and full of joy and peace. Words could not express the delight I felt. This delight increased and increased until I felt I could not contain more.

1 Peter 1: 8: ". . . rejoice with joy unspeakable and full of glory."

Joyfulness reined in heaven. Here there was no sadness, pain, distress, hunger or fatigue in heaven. Heaven was filled with the glory of God.

John 1: 14: "And the word of God became flesh and dwelt among us and we beheld His glory, the glory as of the only begotten of the Father, full of grace and truth."

Usually one can live to seventy or eighty years here on earth, but no one can decide how long we will live.

Psalms 90: 10: "The days of our years are threescore and ten (seventy) . . ."

These years are a short span of time in the eyes of God. Where our soul goes after death is the most important thing in a person's life. Leading to emptiness is working hard for selfish gain. Accepting Jesus Christ as their Lord and Savior was not a concern to them. If they do not repent before death their souls will be tormented in hell without Jesus and for eternity.

Heaven is a good place to live for it is definitely filled with joy and peace. Every nook and cranny shines with the light of God, no stars, sun or moon, just the radiant light of God. By this light, of God, my body was being strengthened.

Even though my loved ones were still on earth, I did not wish to return because I was free from the pain and suffering I had on earth. Oh! The happiness when one is in the realm of happiness cannot be explained.

Jesus held out his hand and told me to take the gift box he was offering me. I accepted and within a split second he was gone but I heard him say "Daughter, come to me and I will show you something, I will help you."

Two angels came up beside me, one on the right and one on the left. I felt no nervousness or discomfort, only calmness and peacefulness. Suddenly my vision seemed to have a 360 degree angle. I was guided by the angels to a road so shiny I could see my reflection. The Bible tells us the roads in heaven are paved with gold.

Revelation 21: 21: ". . . and the streets of the city were paved in pure gold, as it were transparent glass."

After seeing the gold streets I was suddenly transported to a vast plain where very beautiful horses pranced. A big city stood in the middle of the field. Without touching the ground, with my feet, I was drawn towards the city. As the angels escorted me to the city I experienced more intense delight as I drew nearer the city. The walls of the city were very high and of various colors. There were twelve colors which radiated and shone like bright lights.

Revelation 21: 19-20: "The foundation of the wall of the city were adorned with all kinds of precious stones: the first foundation was jasper, the second sapphire, the third chalcedony, the fourth emerald, the fifth sardonyx, the sixth sardius, the seventh chrysolite, the eight beryl, the ninth topaz, the tenth chrysoprase, the eleventh jacinth and the twelfth amethyst."

I stood with wonder and amazement as I stepped through the pearly gates, which looked like it had been sculptured from mother of pearl. There upon the streets were houses with bright, beautiful jeweled houses. Nothing on earth could compare with its beauty and this beautiful sight left me captivated. The city was completely gold, the houses, doors, streets.

Revelation 21: 18: ". . . and the city was pure gold . . ."

familiar faces surrounded me here upon the streets of gold. Parents, grandparents, a younger sister and many, many friends, all I had known on earth but after death had gone on to glory. Each and every one smiled, embraced and welcomed me home.

I then heard the voice of Jesus saying: "This beautiful house is for you and I will let you live here forever." Excitement filled my soul—for this was to be my eternal home.

A most unusual light, towards the center of the city, caught my eye. It was unusually bright, pleasing and delightful beyond measure. My urge was to fall to my knees as I seen the source of this light. But a voice stopped me saying: "You need to return now and declare my glory, power and dominion. You need to warn those who are not saved so they will not have to experience the torments of hell. The day of my coming is soon."

I pleaded with the Lord over and over again because I wanted to stay.

"Lord, I don't want to return."

The earth looked dirty, but I was free and clean here in heaven.

The Lord was adamant that I needed to return to earth. In a loving voice he said: "You have a loving husband who needs you, you have brothers and sisters, so you must return. It is not yet your time." I pleaded with him one more time but he was firm on his decision. "My daughter, be patient and self-controlled, do not grumble, go back. I need you to declare my love and glory."

In Matthew 28: 18: Jesus says, "All power is given unto me in heaven and earth."

Malachi 3: 6 and Hebrews 13: 8 tell us that Jesus changes not and that is the same yesterday, today and forever.

Matthew 5: 48 tells us that our Father which is in heaven is perfect.

Isaiah 45: 23 and Titus 1: 2 tell us that Gods word does not change.

Jeremiah 10: 10 tells us that God is a true and living God.

Deuteronomy 32: 4 tells us God is our rock, that his work is perfect, that he is a God of truth and without iniquity.

1 Timothy 1:17 tells us God is eternal.

Genesis 1: 1, Genesis 2: 4 and Acts 4: 24 tell us God is the creator of heaven and earth.

Isaiah 40: 28, Romans 11: 33 and Job 5: 9 tell us that the ways of the Lord are unsearchable.

Job 11: 7 and Psalms 145: 3 tell us we cannot compare with God; neither can we understand his ability.

John 3: 36 tells us that we can only obtain life only if we believe in Jesus and his resurrection.

John 14: 6 tells us that Jesus is the way, the truth and the life.

Even though the Bible was written thousands of years ago it is still true and reverent. The Bible is a collection of records concerning creation, hell, past and present events. Every word of the Bible is true and it shows the way to salvation is found in Jesus.

I repeat John 14: 6 because it is very important for everyone to know that Jesus said; "I am the way, the truth and the life . . ."

Gods' desire is for everyone to believe in the Lord Jesus Christ to receive salvation and to spend eternity in the lake of fire is not his desire.

When we as Christians die, we go to a better place and our bodies return to dust, we go to a separate place where everything is good and everything is very, very happy *but* for the non-believers there is a place of sadness.

CHAPTER 14

ROM THE PRESENCE OF the Lord the hospital room begins to fill with light. It was so powerful it lit up the whole room with his glory and it was so beautiful to behold. As I was being lifted up I was clad in a white robe.

There was a pair of doors, in front of me, as I arrived at the entrance of heaven. I was awed at what was happening, but God was there along with two angels, who had four wings.

In a language I could not understand one of the angels spoke to me. After they spoke I was given the ability to understand them. Their language was so different, nothing like anything on earth. Opening the immense doors the angels welcomed me in. Oh! So many different, beautiful things. Once inside a perfect peace permeated my heart.

In Philippians 4: 7 it tells us that God would give us peace that surpasses all human understanding; ". . . and the peace of God, which passeth all understanding, shall keep your hearts and minds through Christ Jesus."

A huge tree in the center of paradise caught my eye.

Revelation 2: 7: ". . . To him that overcometh will I give to eat of the tree of life, which is in the midst of the paradise of God."

This tree is a symbol of Jesus because Christ is eternal life. Flowing alongside the tree was a river of crystalline water. This river far surpassed anything I had ever seen on earth; it was so clear and beautiful. I wanted to stay here in this place.

I ask the Lord to let me stay in this place because it was so beautiful and my desire was to stay here and never return to earth.

But the Lord said it was imperative that I return to earth. He told me to give testimony of all the things I have prepared for all those who love me.

I rushed to the river and submerged myself. This river seemed to have a life in itself. The water was deep and many different colored fish swam within it. As I returned to shore I took some of the fish from the water with me, but even out of the water the fish did not die. I was puzzled by this and ask the Lord why. He smiled at me and said that in heaven there is no death, no more crying and no more pain.

Revelation 21: 4: "And God shall wipe away all tears from their eyes; and there shall be no more death, neither sorrow, nor crying, neither shall there be any more pain . . ."

Coming out of this crystalline water I had a desire to go to every place I could find, to touch and experience everything. The things of heaven surprised me so much I wanted to bring them back to earth.

John 7: 38: "He that believeth on me, as the scripture hath said, out of his belly shall flow rivers of living water."

Inside and outside the river the light was normal, for in heaven light did not come from a precise source—everything was just brightly lit up.

Revelation 21: 23: "And the city had no need of the sun, neither of the moon, to shine in it; for the glory of God did lighten it and the Lamb is the light thereof."

CHAPTER 15

EFORE ME WAS A vast area, a very beautiful and wonderful place. Precious stones, gold, emeralds, rubies and diamonds were everywhere and the floor was pure gold.

Continuing on my way I came to a place where there were three large books. The first, a Bible made of gold, including the pages and scriptures.

In Psalms 119: 89 it says: "For ever, O Lord, thy word is settles in heaven."

God's word is eternal and it remains in heaven.

The second book was larger than the Bible. This book was open and an angel was writing inside this book. With the Lord by my side I came closer to see what was being written. In this book the angel was writing everything that was happening on earth, the date, the hour, everything was written there. This recording of events was done so the Word of God could be fulfilled.

Revelation 20:12: "And I saw the dead, small and great stand before God and the books were opened and another book was opened, which is the Book of

Life and the dead were judged out of those things which were written in the books, according to their works."

Whether good or bad, the angels had written everything.

Daniel 12: 1: "Everyone whose name is written in God's book will be saved."

As I continued I came to the place where the third book was. This book was larger than the last two and was sitting across pillars. The columns in heaven were wonderfully braided and were made of precious stones. Some of the pillars were made of diamonds, others of pure emeralds, and others of pure gold and still yet others were made from a combination of different types of stones. This made me realize God really is the owner of all things.

Haggai 2: 8: "The silver is Mine and the gold is Mine saith the Lord of hosts."

God is absolutely rich and owns all the riches in the world. The world in all its fullness belongs to God and it is His desire to give it to all who ask in faith.

Psalms 2: 8: "If you ask me, I will give you the nations . . . for an inheritance."

The book I was now looking at was so huge that I had to literally walk back and forth on the pages. The language inside this book was hard to read because it was not an earthly language, it was totally heavenly. But the Holy Ghost came upon me and gave me the grace to understand it. With the help of the Holy

Ghost I was able to read through the pages as if it was my own language. I could see my name was written there. The name that was written in the book was not my earthly name. This name was new so that the word of God could be fulfilled when it said that he would give me a new name that no one else knows.

Revelation 2: 17: ". . . I will also give to each one who wins victory a white stone with a name written on it. No one knows this name except the one who receives it."

Revelation 3: 12: ". . . I will also write on them my new name."

Those who win the victory will be dressed in white clothes like them. And I not erase their names from the Book of Life, but I will say they belong to me before my Father and before the angels."

While in heaven I was able to pronounce my heavenly name but once I was back in my earthly body this name was stripped from my memory and my heart. Once I regained my place in heaven I will again have my heavenly name. The Word of God is eternal and must be fulfilled.

Revelation 1: 8: "I am Alpha and Omega, the beginning and the end . . ."

Family and friends, I implore you, from the deepest recesses of my heart, *do not* let any one seize or hold force or remove the place the Father has ready for you. Heaven has many wonderful things that can't be expressed by words. God is waiting for you and this is certain. However it is only the person who perseveres until the end that will be saved.

Mark 13: 13: ". . . those people who keep their faith until the end will be saved."

TREE OF LIFE:

Revelation 2: 7: ". . . To those who win the victory I will give the right to eat the fruit from the tree of life, which is in the Garden of Eden."

I saw white horses in a distance.

Revelation 19: 11: "And I saw heaven opened and behold a white horse; and he that sat upon him was Faithful and True . . ."

I went up to the horses and began to pet them and upon one of them, the Lord allowed me to ride. During this ride I experienced peace, freedom, love and holiness that could only be felt in this beautiful place. In this beautiful place I was allowed to enjoy everything the Lord had prepared for me. The crown of life was ready to be taken by me.

2 Timothy 4: 8: ". . . there is laid up for me the crown of righteousness, which the Lord, the righteous judge, will give to me on that day . . ."

The banquet table was exquisitely prepared and was without end. Delicious food had already been set for me and all those that will be invited to the Wedding of the Lamb. The angels offered me a white cloth, to be used as a cloak that the Lord had prepared. The Bible tells us that we have to receive the kingdom of God like little children.

Matthew 18: 3: ". . . Except ye be converted and become as little children, ye shall not enter the kingdom of God."

During my stay in heaven I was like a little child, enjoying everything, the flowers, the trees, the animals and much more. The residence of people was something to see and I was allowed to go inside the residences.

As I went on I came to a place full of children. In the midst Jesus was playing with them. Jesus really enjoyed spending time and interacting with the children and he gave each of them quality time. As I came near to Jesus side I ask him if these were the children born on earth. With a sad look in his eyes he told me that these children were the ones who had been aborted on earth. When he spoke these words, my heart sank.

God has already forgiven your sins, now you have to learn to forgive yourself.

Ephesians 4: 32:" . . . as God in Christ forgave you."

Revelation 4: 1: ". . . behold a door was opened in heaven . . ."

As the door opened I seen a valley a valley of flowers that were beautiful and the smell was exquisite. Looking at the flowers I realized they were unique for each petal was different, genuine and each had a remarkable color. Nothing happened as I tried to pick one. Jesus came over to my side and told me everything had to be done in love. Reaching down Jesus touched the flower and it surrendered itself to him. Jesus than gave me the flower and I carried it as we walked along. As long as I had the flower in my hand the scent stayed with me.

As we walked along we came to a beautiful set of doors. These doors were very showy with precious stones engraved in them and as the doors were opened there was a lot of scurrying as preparations were being made. There was a group carrying rolls of shining white cloth on their shoulders, while others carried spindles of golden thread and yet others were taking plates with something like shields sitting upon them. Not one person was idle—each was scurrying around with effort.

My question to God was; "Why is everyone in such a hurry?"

In answer to my question he commanded a man to come near. This man carried a roll of cloth upon his shoulder and as he came near he looked reverently at the Lord.

"Why are you carrying the cloth upon your shoulder?' the Lord asks.

Puzzled the man said; "Lord, you know what this cloth is for. This cloth is used to make the robes of the redeemed, the robes for the Great Bride."

I felt joy and peace as I heard this statement.

Revelation 19: *: "And to her was granted that she should be arrayed in fine linen, clean and white: for the fine linen is the righteousness of saints."

Coming out of this place I felt more peace because God was making something beautiful and nice for me. Because you are important to him he has the place and time for you. Every detail in heaven I etched on my mind. To God every object gave glory to God and each and everything had a life in itself.

The next place I came to had millions of children of all ages. When these children saw Jesus coming they ran up to him wanting to hug him, to feel his love because he was their passion and to each and everyone Jesus was their passion. As Jesus reacted with the children tears came to my eyes at the way he lavished his love on them, kissing them and holding each one close.

By angels children were brought to Jesus wrapped in linen. He would hold them tenderly in his arms touching and caressing them. Before handing them back to the angels he would bestow a kiss upon their forehead. The angels would then take the babies to a special place in heaven.

"Lord, why are there so many babies in the special place? Are they being sent to earth?"

As I looked into his eyes, tears begin to fall as he said: "No child, these babies will not be sent to earth. These are the ones that were aborted on earth by parents who didn't want them. These are my children and I love them." My body trembled that I had to ask the Lord such a question.

Another stop was a place with small mountains and Jesus came dancing. Ahead of him were people dressed in white robes and with green olive branches lifted up in their hands. As the branches were waved in the air, oil was released. By God great things have been prepared for you.

Before I accepted Christ as my Savior I made mistakes and sinned like everyone else.

Isaiah 65: 19: "I will rejoice in Jerusalem and joy in my people . . ."

CHAPTER 16

*O*N HEAVEN I SAW wonderful things that were written about in the Bible.

1 Corinthians 2: 9: ". . . Eye hath not seen, nor ear heard, neither have entered into the heart of man, the things which God has prepared for them that love him."

There were so many spectacular and wonderful things to see and feel within the glory of God.

Heaven was divided into four sections. One section was for toddlers' two to four. These children grow up. The children were educated by angels in a school where the word of God was taught. The teachers (angels) taught worship, songs and how to glorify the Lord Jesus. Upon Jesus arrival, in the classroom, there was immense joy for his smile filled the whole room and the children ran up to greet him. In the center of the children was Mary, the mother of Jesus and she was so beautiful. She was not upon a throne nor was there anyone worshipping her, for in heaven Mary was just one of the women. Like all human beings she had to win her salvation. She wore a white robe with a golden belt around her waist and her beautiful hair hung down to her waist. Some people on earth worship Mary, but this is so wrong.

In John 14: 6 Jesus tells us; "I am the way, the truth and the life, no one comes to the Father but by me."

The only way you can enter the kingdom of heaven is through Jesus of Nazareth.

There was no sun—no moon.

Revelation 22: 5: "And there shall be no night there; and they need no candle, neither light of the sun; for the Lord God giveth them light . . ."

I could see Gods glory but for me to explain the celestial things I saw and the perfection of our Maker is impossible. Nothing can compare to heaven. During my visit to heaven I wanted to touch and feel everything and feel the soft wind caressing my face because it was all so wonderful.

In the center of the sky was an immense cross made of pure gold. This cross symbolized the death of Jesus upon the cross.

With Jesus by my side we continued walking and, oh, how fascinating it was to walk with him. Many of the people on earth have the misconception that the Lord is just waiting for us to sin, so he can punish us. *That is not reality.* The side of Jesus I saw was one of a friend, one who cries when we cry.

Proverbs 18: 24: ". . . there is a friend that sticketh closer than a brother."

Jesus Christ is a God of love, compassion and mercy. By his hand he helped me continue in the way of salvation.

God tells us in Revelation 21: 27: "Nothing unclean and no one who does shameful things or tell lies will ever go into it. Only those whose names are written in the Lamb's book of Life will enter the city."

Nothing unclean or anyone practicing immorality and falsehood shall enter into heaven, only the ones whose names are written in the Lamb's book of Life. Only the brave ones take hold of the kingdom of heaven.

2 Corinthians 5: 10: ". . . we must all stand before God to be judged. Each of us will receive what we should get—good or bad—for the things we did in the earthly body."

In the kingdom of heaven I could see New Jerusalem that the Bible tells us about in John 14: 2: "In my Father's house are many mansions: if it were not so, I would have told you. I go to prepare a place for you."

I was allowed to see and enter the city, so real and wonderful. Each house had the owners name written in front. New Jerusalem is not inhabited but is ready for us. I seen the inside of the houses and all that was inside, but when I left the city, the things I saw were forgotten, the memory taken from me. I remember the columns of the house were plated with precious metals and more precious metals encrusted in them and there was gold in the pillars.

The gold is like the Bible describes—transparent and shiny. Revelation 21: 21: ". . . as it were transparent glass."

Nothing on earth could compare to it.

The Lord then led me to a place that was full of containers. In these containers were crystallized tears from men and women of God that they had shed on earth. Not tears of complaints but of people that were in the presence of God—tears of repentance—tears of gratitude. The Lord said these tears were kept as precious treasures in heaven.

Psalms 56: 8: "You have recorded my troubles. You have kept a list of my tears. Aren't they in your records?"

Another place I visited, while in heaven, was a place that had many, many angels. There were many different types of angels in heaven, but this place was different. In this place there was one specific type of angels. For each of us, Jesus has assigned a specific angel. The angel that is assigned to us will remain with us our entire life. Jesus gave me the opportunity to meet my angel and to see her characteristics but God told me that I was not allowed to reveal these things to others.

Psalms 91:11: "For he gives his angels orders regarding you, to protect you wherever you go."

Farther on I came to a place full of flowers. Some of these were open, beautiful and radiant whereas some were droopy and still others were shriveled.

"What is the meaning of these flowers?" I ask Jesus.

"Each and every person is like a flower." To demonstrate the point he picked a radiant flower and held it out for me to see. "This flower shows the close relationship that you have with me." Laying the radiant flower down he picked up a droopy one and said, "Look, this person is down because they are having a trial or difficulty. There is something in their life that is interrupting the communion between them and me. Do you know, my child, what I do with these flowers when they are down in order to make them brilliant and healthy?" Without me saying anything he took the flower in his hands and said, "I shed tears over them and raise them up. As his tears fell upon the flower, it once again had life and the color returned.

The shriveled flower he picked up and threw it into the fire saying, "Look, this person once knew me and then walked away from me. Dying without me this person will be thrown into the fire."

Matthew 13: 42: "And shall cast them into the furnace of fire . . ."

John 15: 6: "and cast them into the fire and they are burned."

In the distance I saw a castle but no one dared get close to it. I believe that is what the Scriptures talks about in Revelation 22: 1, "And he shewed me a pure river of water of life, clear as crystal, proceeding out of the throne of God and of the Lamb." My belief was that the castle was located near the presence and throne of God.

During my time in heaven I experienced so much joy in my heart. I had peace that passeth all understanding.

Philippians 4: 7: "and the peace of God, which passeth all understanding, shall keep your hearts and minds through Jesus Christ."

I understood 1 Peter 1: 4, "To an inheritance incorruptible and undefiled and that fadeth not away, reserved in heaven for you."

Luke 22: 30: "That ye may eat and drink at my table in my kingdom and sit on thrones judging the twelve tribes of Israel."

In a marvelous place God allowed me to see the most beautiful reception hall, that I thought could not exist anywhere in the universe. Another thing that did not exist on earth was pure gold and precious stones. There was a giant throne with two chairs made of gold and precious stone. A table that seemed to have no end was in front of the throne and it was covered with a very beautiful white tablecloth. My thought was 'How could they find a tablecloth to fit table?' on this table was the most exquisite and purified food. The taste of this food was beyond anything I had ever tasted on earth.

EVERYONE, listen!!! You can't imagine all the things that are ready in the kingdom of heaven and what God has already prepared for you.

1 Corinthians 2: 9: ". . . eye hath not seen nor ear heard, neither have entered into the heart of man,

the things which God has prepared for them that love him."

I was allowed to see the bread, the *manna* that was spoken of in the Scriptures. Manna is a small white seed and it tasted like wafers made with honey. The Lord allowed me to taste so many things that don't exist on earth.

All these are waiting for me as my incorruptible inheritance in the kingdom of heaven. When we inherit the kingdom of heaven we will enjoy delicious, exquisite foods. On each side of the table were chairs and each chair had a name written on it. No earthly names but the heavenly names that nobody else knew but the person who was given that name.

Luke 10: 20: "But you should not be happy because the spirits obey you but because your name is written in heaven. A sad thing was some of the chairs had been removed because there were men and women who tired of serving God and their names were erased from the Lamb's book of Life and are now sent away from the wedding supper of the Lamb.

In heaven, all of us will rejuvenate and be healthy again and young again.

Beware!!! The coming of the Lord is approaching quickly.

CHAPTER 17

A BIG, GOLDEN, BEAUTIFUL BEING appeared suddenly before me. With a snap of his finger, I was lifted from my bed and drawn into a beautiful and bright light. I remember feeling weightless and the feeling was beyond explaining. I was flat on my back as I traveled through the light. This being that appeared before me seemed to be speaking softly to me, although I could not understand the words, his presence profoundly comforted me.

This beautiful being took me into a beautiful garden. The trees were gigantic and each blade of grass had a diamond, a jewel and an emerald inside of it, but as I walked upon the grass, it was as soft as cotton. The grass was absolutely pure and light with color. I stood pushing the blades of grass aside and as I did there was a river right in front of me, running from my right to my left. I looked up from the river and saw a beautiful stone built wall that stood extremely high. Beautiful music came from behind the walls. Behind this wall people were talking and worshipping. Here, in heaven, the sound of people talking and worshipping is much pure than anything on earth. I came near the wall but could not see inside. From inside I could hear the melodious sounds of people singing and worshipping, so I knew I was not alone.

As I walked along this lane there were colors on both sides. OH!! They were such brilliant colors, such a kaleidoscope of colors. No artist could ever reproduce these colors, no matter how hard they tried, because they were so bright. The light of the Holy Spirit surrounded me and was caring for me. In my entire life I had never felt so good or safe.

I came upon a river which seemed to be dancing to music and it was wonderful. The river was so crystal clear I could see to the bottom of this wonderful river and I could clearly see the stones on the bottom. This river seemed to come from a giant, beautiful building and the rainbow colors from the flowing waters looked like liquid diamonds. The angels were singing and on the other side I could see my younger sister, my grandfather and a niece.

Some force was pulling me back away from the river because I wanted to cross over and be with my family, to embrace them in my arms. Across the river I also saw children running. There were three groups of children. The first group was children who died from wars, accidents, cancer and other deadly diseases. The second group was children who had been aborted and were sent back to the Lord. Tears filled God's eyes as he spoke of these aborted ones. The third group was children the Lord had sent to so called *church people,* who only listened to the ways of the world and then secretly went and had an abortion. These children were sent back to the Lord.

Two Warnings:

The first warning is to <u>Repent.</u>

The other warning: Stop holding grudges and bad thoughts against God. He told me that; "There are so many people holding things against me as if I sinned. There are church people who have not forgiven me because they have not gotten what they wanted in the time frame they wanted. People are holding grudges against me in their hearts. I cannot bless them until they ask for forgiveness."

If you feel this way and want to make amends with God say to God from the depth of your heart and with meaning say; 'God, I am sorry how I felt about you.'

God has sent numerous warnings to people to repent but they go on living their own way. Instead of seeking God's face, they chase after money and other materialistic things.

Hebrews 3: 12: "Take heed, brethren, lest there be in any of you an evil heart of unbelief, in departing from the living God."

Hebrews 4: 12: "For the Word of God is quick and powerful and sharper than any two-edged sword, piercing even to the dividing asunder of the soul and spirit and of the joints and marrow and is a discerner of the thoughts and intents of the heart."

1 Corinthians 14: 1: ". . . desire spiritual gifts . . ."

1 Corinthians 2: 9: ". . . Eye hath not seen, nor ear heard, neither have entered into the heart of man, the things which God hath prepared for them that love him."

1 Corinthians 12: 8-10 tells us of the wonderful spiritual gifts God has for us.

In Ephesians 4: 4 God tells us: "There is one body and one Spirit . . ."

Every day do an inventory on yourself to make sure you are staying within the perimeter. Get on your knees and pray to God.

Say: "God I want you to use me because I know what's awaiting me."

Before it's too late souls have to be warned.

Romans 8: 28: "And we know that all things work together for good to them that love God, to them who are called according to his purpose."

When we are in a bad situation we don't necessarily believe it, but I can assure you *God is in control* and will work everything out for good. At the end of the day it's about God, not us, it's all about him.

All the broken pieces of your life are nothing more than a beautiful mosaic of your future. We can pick up the pieces of our life and put it together to create a beautiful new picture under the guidance of the Holy

Spirit—or because of your madness at God, you throw it all away. There is so much more than being reborn. There is much more to being a true child of God than what we are.

There is a treasure to be found in brokenness.

In order for us to have the peace of God than we have to die within ourselves. It is free to all but not everyone takes it.

Cry out to God: "Father, I am calling out to you for I want the peace that passeth all understanding."

Make a choice today. Do not be full of yourself. *Me, Myself and I* are more difficult to unlearn.

No matter how much money you have—only God has the power over life and death.

Exodus 20: 21 tells us that God was in a dark cloud. ". . . Moses drew near unto the thick darkness where God was." God is in your difficult situation.

Are you there for those around you? Are you one step away from somebody needing help, or are you on the sidelines shouting 'I'll pray for you?'

I realized that I wasn't Jesus' hands and never had been which was a shock to me, to realize this.

Proverbs 18: 21: "Death and life are in the power of the tongue: and they that love it shall eat the fruit thereof."

This verse in Proverbs 18: 21 tells us that life and death lies within the power of the tongue. Anyone who uses the tongue shall reap the rewards of his words. It says shall, not might.

John 10: 10 is a beautiful verse that says: "The thief cometh not, but for to steal and to kill and to destroy: I am come that they might have life and that they might have it more abundantly."

The Word of God teaches me that he speaks to me through dreams, visions and His word.

Have you noticed how many people can pronounce death, over their marriages, their finances, children and more? Church people, they call themselves. Watch what you say and think what you say. Life and death is within the power of the tongue and you shall reap the rewards of your words.

God answers those who seek him. God said to me; 'Child, take off your shoes, for you are on holy ground.'

What an experience this was, for me, to be in the presence of the Lord.

God had a question for me and that was; 'Do you believe that my Son already paid the price on the cross for you?'

'Yes, Yes, I definitely do!!'

In my spirit I saw how Jesus endured the 38 stripes (lashes) for me. With the last one, the 38th, I couldn't see a human being anymore, all I seen was a lump of flesh. Through the Spirit of God I saw Jesus beaten beyond recognition by his enemies.

In the temple I seen the veil ripped din two— so thick no human could have torn it and so unbelievably high.

God called me by name and said 'Holly Jo, this is humanly impossible. There's the veil and it's open.'

Through the spirit I saw the outer court and center. In the center was a bowl of water. God said to me, 'Come, my child, and wash your hands so you may enter into the holiest of places. 'Come inside, for the veil was rent for you to enter.'

I entered the holiest of places, barefoot, meeting God there.

'It is now complete,' he told me. For the first time in my life I experienced what Jesus did for me on the cross.

1 Corinthians 1: 31: ". . . If someone wants to brag, he should brag about the Lord."

The most amazing thing happened—suddenly I was in the throne room of God and the light was extremely bright. I find it hard to explain this light for it was the kind that could shine through your bones.

'What is this amazing light?' I ask.

1 John 1: 5: ". . . God is light and in him is no darkness at all."

Luke 18: 27: ". . . The things which are impossible with men are possible with God."

Hebrews 11: 1: "Now faith is the substance of things hoped for, the evidence of things not seen."

Hope is available to every child of God. Here's your title deed. Everything you hope for—tell me. What is your hope? Because here is your deed, take it.

I had never realized that God was such a reality.

God said to me: "My child everyday that you break bread, you die with me. Every time you take a drink of my blood, you rise with me, because I am the Bread of Life. He who eats my flesh and drinks my blood will be one with me."

Ezekiel tells us that we will be filled and I could feel how I was being filled with the Spirit of God.

Ezekiel 11: 19: "And I will give them one heart and I will put a new spirit within you . . ."

The scriptures tell us how streams of living water shall flow from your inner being.

Psalms 1: 3 tells us how we will be like a tree planted next to a river, one that bears fruit at the right time.

"And he shall be like a tree planted by the rivers of water, that bringeth forth his fruit in his season; his leaf also shall not wither . . ."

This I could feel because I had died in myself.

A valuable lesson was learned. It doesn't help to look at or to listen to circumstances. Jesus said to me; "Don't fear—look at me. Look at me and keep believing."

God has a vision for you and me.

Abraham was asked by god to sacrifice his son, Isaac, but because of Abraham's faith God provided a ram.

Why is not my ram coming, you may ask? Maybe because you are not sacrificing your problem to the Lord. It is very well possible that you are holding the ram (problem) in your lap. God is waiting for you to be obedient: to sacrifice your problem so he can send you the ram. He has a plan for everything, our finances, our marriages that are failing and every other problem we have. *Jesus is the plan*—give your problem to the Lord today for your ram is ready.

The Lord says he needs your faith.

Mark 11: 22 tells us to, ". . . Have faith in God."

If we do not have faith in God's promises, than those promises cannot come true. God's promise plus my faith equals a miracle.

We cannot sit back and receive our miracle; we must take the first step in faith, which usually is the most difficult part.

Isaiah 30: 21: "And thine ears shall hear a word behind thee, saying, This is the way, walk ye in it, when ye turn to the right and when ye turn to the left."

God's peace will meet you. That is how you will know you are in the will of God. Take the first step.

The only ones that will enter the kingdom of God are the pure in heart, his obedient children.

Matthew 5: 8: "Blessed are the pure in heart: for they shall see God."

Many call themselves Christians but do not live by God's word. Some think going to church once a week is enough, but never read God's word and go about doing their own thing and pursuing worldly things. Even some who do read their Bible don't know Christ as their personal Savior and don't have Christ in their heart.

Lord, I don't want to risk making this painful journey, just to end up in heaven and not be ready.

Revelation 3: 15-16: "I know what you do, that you are not hot or cold. I wish that you were hot or cold. But because you are lukewarm—neither hot or cold—I am ready to spit you out of my mouth.

Revelation 3: 18-19 "I advise you to buy from me gold made pure in fire so you can be truly rich. Buy from me white clothes so you can be clothed and so you can cover your nakedness. Buy from me medicine to put on your eyes so you can truly see. Correct and punish those whom I love. So be eager to do right and change your hearts and lives."

Jesus said; "I will counsel you, come and purchase from me."

Purchase means that there is a price involved, but Jesus already paid the ultimate price. There is nothing else he can do for you. He paid it all, bearing upon his body 38 lashes, now it's your turn and mine.

Jesus went up to heaven to sit on the right hand of his Father and left us the Holy Ghost.

John 20: 22: ". . . Receive ye the Holy Ghost."

Jesus will comfort and guide you. He's your advocate, your everything.

Everyone doesn't experience God. Why? Because your sin is a wall, keeping you away from God so that you do not hear the voice of the Holy Spirit of God.

It's inside you.

CHAPTER 18

A s I awoke the next morning I ask, "Are you here Holy Spirit?" The answer came back and said; "I am here with you and I love you so much. I am here with you. My child, I want to walk this road with you and guide you in all my glory."

Isaiah 58: 11: "And the Lord will guide thee continually . . ."

my spirit became exalted. First you have to die and then God fills you with his Holy Spirit. The reason we don't get abundance or victory is because we are too full of ourselves. 'Stay with me, my dear precious child;' God said to me.

Revelation 19: 11-13 tells us that he was riding a white horse and his eyes were as flames of fire. "Then I saw heaven opened and there before me was a white horse. The rider on the horse is called Faithful and True, and he is right when he judges and makes war. His eyes are like burning fire and on his head are many crowns. He has a name written on him, which no one but himself knows. He is dressed in a robe dripped in blood and his name is the Word of God."

I was told once again by God to stay in his word, stay with me and I will stay with you.

Some people have given their problems to the Lord, but because their prayers weren't answered in their time, they took their problems back.

Once you and God have become one, he will never again let go of you. In the scriptures it teaches us that God wants to sign a covenant of peace with us.

Numbers 25: 12: ". . . I give unto him my covenant of peace."

This covenant means that everything that is God's is mine and all my shortcomings, my hurt and my pain are his. Everything that is his, his kingdom, everything that is God's becomes mine and I become one with him. He tell me that I will lack nothing, nothing at all, but that he will have to start kneading me which might hurt a little. Then he said he would flatten me on all sides, put me in a pan and put me in the oven. The oven will not be the nicest place to be but might be the best place for me.

Are you useful to God or are you still in your shell?

With excitement, I thought—If that's what God wants, that is exactly what he will get.

John 15: 7 tells us that; "If ye abide in me, and my words abide in you, ye shall ask what ye will and it shall be done unto you."

Why don't we always get what we want? The answer to that is because we still are not one with God. Being one with God asks you to die within yourself first. A lot of people are not prepared to pay the price. You don't have to pay anything; all you have to do is say; "Yes, Lord and die within yourself."

1 John 1: 12: "He that hath the Son hath life . . ."

Manna is God's word. The word of God must be like a bubbling fountain of living water. The more you have of it, the more you are being fed from the inside. The living waters will start flowing from inside you.

What is coming out of your mouth? Is it streams of living water or streams of bitterness that are eating you up from the inside?

Being the bride of God asks of you to be pure and bathed in his blood. Are you a bride or just an acquaintance of God?

Jesus didn't die on the cross to give you religion; he died on the cross to give you a relationship with the living supernatural God. Praise God for dying on the cross because he did that so you can have life and life in abundance.

John 10: 10; ". . . I am come that they might have life and that they might have it more abundantly."

Jesus did this so we could face tomorrow.

I love you so much and want to thank you for the Holy Spirit. I can now open my arms wide, unlocking the door to my heart. The door that only has a handle on the inside. I'm doing this so that you

can see what's going on. Spirit of God—fill me. Reveal to me everything that is bad in my life so that I may rectify them. Lord, reveal any bitterness in my heart, the selfishness, the me, myself and I attitude. I want to choose to die with you and to rise with you.

Life or death!! Today I choose life. I choose life, a life in abundance with you.

Deuteronomy 30: 19: ". . . I have set before you life and death . . ."

holy Spirit, remove anything that must go. I am at the point in my life where there is nothing left and for that I praise and honor you.

'Lord God, come and fill me with your loving liquid love. Pour it out in my spirit, Lord. Keep pouring until it overflows.'

Because Christ is alive I can face obstacles and problems.

Sacrifice anything in your life, such as your marriage, children, finances, and business—*do it*, right there where you are.

Matthew 7: 21: "Not every one that saith unto me, Lord, Lord shall enter into the kingdom of heaven . . ."

Everyone cannot enter through the gates of heaven. There is gold bridge you have to cross. The door into the gateway is huge and has pearls embedded in it. Once inside there is a wedding banquet.

Standing around were people with their heads hanging low—dejected and hopeless.

'Who are these people, Lord?'

'They are disobedient Christians;' was his reply.

I then ask him; 'How long will they stand in this dead, empty place?'

'Forever, my daughter. The only ones who will enter the kingdom of God are the pure in heart, my obedient children. Many call themselves Christians but they do not live by my word. I am here in all my glory to guide you.'

The Lord than said to me; 'Child, you and I are now one, come and have communion with me, come my precious child.'

Get rid of your pride and being grand. Put your hands in the air and say; 'Lord, here am I. I desire to receive your Holy Spirit. I confess today that Jesus Christ died for me and rose again. He is my Savior and my salvation. I announce openly that God's spirit lives in me and that he will guide me in everything I need. I thank you, Lord, that I will lack nothing, for I am now one with you, dear Lord. Forever will I hear your voice? I thank you for the power in my life.'

If there is someone who is reading this that hasn't accepted the Lord as their Savior and want to be saved, say this prayer; "In the name of the Father, I accept you Jesus. Thank you for dying on the cross for me then rising from the dead for me. I thank you, dear Lord, for the circumstances that has brought me to this point in my life where I realize I am nothing without you. Please come soon and fetch me for I am ready."

1 Corinthians 5: 21: "Christ had no sin, but God made him become sin so that in Christ we could become right with God."

Romans 3: 22-23: "God makes people right with himself through their faith in Jesus Christ. For all have sinned and come short of the glory of God."

CHAPTER 19

I LEFT THE HOUSE AFTER I had gotten in a quarrel with my husband. During this quarrel I had used some profane language and some other nasty things. As I drove around town, with no particular destination, my thought was on how to revenge instead of thinking how I could rectify the situation. Driving erratically through the streets my heart filled with hate against the man I had promised to love and cherish. My thoughts were so intense on my hatred that I did not see the eighteen wheeler in front of me and as a result I was in a severe accident. Everything in my life was to change because of this accident.

In the blink of an eye there were two angels by my side and they lifted me from the wreckage. Ever so gracefully and tenderly we flew though time and space and before long we were at the gates of heaven. Walking through the gate I seen multitudes of people and they seemed ageless and race less. None appeared to be young, middle-aged, or old and none had any racial characteristics. All were focused on the bright light, worshipping in harmony and they would all lift their hands and bow as if some unseen power guided them. One of the angels, that had guided me to heaven said to me; 'the ones worshipping there with God are the human beings who while on earth served God and had their faith focused on Christ Jesus and lived righteously.' The angels took me to a mansion that God had prepared for those whom he would righteous on the last day.

Isaiah 33: 15-16: "He that walketh righteously and speaketh righteously . . . he shall dwell on high."

The mansion was endless and was without height or depth and it moved continually and in some way the room revolved. The floors glowed with a supernatural light and the mansion was made of something that looked like transparent glass. There didn't seem to be anyone in the mansion, but I heard beautiful singing. I wondered where the music was coming from. One of the angels pointed to the flowers that were swaying and singing praises to God. I was told by the angels that the mansions were ready, but the saints of God were not. Jesus is delaying his coming because Christians in the church are not ready yet.

After seeing all I was suppose to see the angel guided me to the gates of hell. When the angel lifted his hand and let it fall, hell's gates opened and immediately I heard the awful sounds of people screaming and weeping. Total darkness surrounded hell, but the bright light from the angel made it possible for me to see numerous groups of people in anguish. I was told by the angel that there are three definite groups that went through endless cycles of torment forever, reaping in hell what they had sown on earth. The first group was a gruesome sight. It was of people eating their own flesh, vomiting it onto the ground, at which time it would fly back into their bodies and the cycle would be continued over and over. The angel explained to me that these were people who had eaten flesh as an occult practice.

The second group were people who had stolen land from others while they lived on earth, now they were digging rock-hard ground with their bare hands, which left their hands blistered and bleeding.

The third group was the adulterers and fornicators.

Jude verse 7: "Even as Sodom and Gomorrha and the cities about the cities about them in like manner, giving themselves over to fornication and going after strange flesh, are set forth for an example, suffering the vengeance of eternal fire."

The people in this third group were endlessly mutilating their sexual organs, which after they destroyed them, would be regenerated and the mutilation would begin again.

God declares in the scriptures that he will repay every person according to his or her deeds and he promises that everyone will reap precisely what they have sown.

Galatians 6: 7: ". . . whatsoever a man soweth, that shall he also reap."

There are many different types of torture in hell, all the people in hell writhed in agony under an unseen force that would repeatedly wrench them. Every person in hell were crying, shouting and gnashing their teeth.

The angel made a statement that sent my head reeling and it was this; 'If your record is to be called here, you will no doubt be thrown into hell.' immediately, I defended myself saying; 'I am a child of God and I serve him with all my heart.' In the hands of the angel, a Bible appeared and he read from Matthew 5: 22: ". . . If you are angry with a brother or sister, you will be judged. If you say bad things to a brother or sister, you will be judged by the council. And if you call someone a fool, you will be in danger of the fire of hell."

I knew I was guilty of the angry words spoken to my husband. The angel reminded me that Jesus promised that God will not forgive our sins if we do not forgive others.

Matthew 6: 14-15: ". . . if you forgive others for their sins, your Father in heaven will also forgive you for your sins. But if you don't forgive others, your Father in heaven will not forgive you."

Only the ones who are merciful will obtain mercy.

Matthew 5: 7: "Blessed are the merciful, for they shall obtain mercy."

The angel looked in squarely in the eyes and said; "Holly Jo, the prayer that you prayed as you were dying has no effect because you refused to forgive your husband, even though he attempted to reconcile before your accident. I stood there dumbfounded, realizing that if my number was called, hell would be my home.

Forgive those you have wronged. Obeying the commandments of Jesus regarding forgiveness and walking in love towards each other, as well as the rest of his commandments is very important.

Do not listen to false teachers that tell you that holiness is not essential to ultimately gaining eternal life.

Matthew 7: 21 says "Not everyone that saith to me. Lord, Lord, shall enter into the kingdom of heaven, but he that doeth the will of my Father which is in heaven."

Once again *do not* listen to teachers who say that if you are saved you are guaranteed that you will always be saved. Even Jesus closest disciples were warned in Matthew 24:1-3 of the possibility of them not being ready and being cast into hell. Also read Matthew 24: 42 and verse 46.

If I expect God to forgive me, I must forgive others.

Ask yourself this question; 'Am I ready to stand before Jesus, sincere and blameless?'

Yes, there really is a heaven and everyone needs to prepare for it. It is authentic and real, just as the Holy Scriptures describes it.

John 3: 16 tells us; "For God so loved the world that he gave his only begotten Son, that whosoever believeth in him should not perish but have everlasting life."

What that means is; God loved you enough that he made a way for your sins to be forgiven, washed away, so at that moment when you take your last breath and you are standing before God, your creator, it's not God casting you away for all eternity into a place called hell. Instead its God ushering you into his holy presence for all eternity in a place called heaven.

PLEASE!!!!PLEASE!!!! Do not delay in making your decision for the Lord. **LOOK!!!** God knows your heart and he is not concerned with your words as he is with the attitude of your heart.

My prayer is for you to believe in God who sent his only son to die on the cross for you because of his great love and compassion.

Look towards heaven with anticipation in a way that reveals intense truth in your life as you move forward in your personal relationship with God.